MW01298103

PRAYERS THAT GET ANSWERS

Prayers Get the Response of Heaven
Volume 1

DR. PAT AKINDUDE

Copyright © 2013 by Dr. Pat Akindude

Prayers That Get Answers
Prayers Get the Response of Heaven
by Dr. Pat Akindude

Printed in the United States of America

ISBN 9781626978256

All rights reserved solely by the author. The author guarantees all contents are original and do not infringe upon the legal rights of any other person or work. No part of this book may be reproduced in any form without the permission of the author. The views expressed in this book are not necessarily those of the publisher.

Scripture quotations taken from the King James Version (KJV) – *public domain*

www.xulonpress.com

ENDORSEMENTS

D r. Pat Akindude is one of the most insightful and anointed teachers on prayer in the world. This book is a "must read" if you want to learn how to pray prayers that get results.

Steve Austin, Sr. Dir., Pastoral Care & Christian Education, Lakewood Church

Change your life with prayer. Let this book teach you to pray effectively. Dr. Pat prays powerfully, with full anointing. In this book, she decrees and takes dominion and authority over the enemy who is trying to destroy our relationship with the Father. Model your prayers after these and get answers from Him.

Mike Marburger, Author and Servant, driven to prayer

DEDICATION

I dedicate this book first to the Lᴏʀᴅ our God, whose mighty power knows no limitation. To the Lᴏʀᴅ, who saw fit to save me and call me into the ministry to bring His Word to His loving people.

I dedicate this book to my husband, Dr. James Akindude, for his love and support.

I dedicate this book to our three wonderful children.

I dedicate this book to all my "Lunch Date With Jesus" family.

PREFACE

This book is a product of my own journey with God—from getting saved, to Him teaching me to live a life of victory and empowerment through effective prayer. There are so many believers who are hurting and living in bondage, and they do not know how to pray effectively using the Word of God. This book contains many prayer points, which will help you be an overcomer and be victoriously blessed in all areas of life.

As the leader of a daily prayer line with people calling in from all over the world, and as the director of intercessory prayer, for Lakewood Church, one of the largest churches in the world, God is showing me strategic ways to pray with the scriptures and get results.

The most powerful prayer we can pray is praying in agreement with the Word of God and personalizing it, as it relates to our issues. The Word of God cannot return to Him void, it must prosper in that for which it is sent—*Isaiah 55:11*. Heaven responds to our prayer, especially when it is releasing the Word. God listens and causes angels to respond to His Word. One power that the devil cannot resist is the Word of God. When Jesus was tempted, He kept saying to the devil, "*...it is written."—Matthew 4:1-11*. Prayer changes things, and brings the power of God into action on our behalf.

TABLE OF CONTENTS

INTRODUCTION

In prayer, we can come to God anytime, anywhere, and expect to receive an answer. In 1992, I was pregnant with our youngest son Johnny. There were some challenges with the pregnancy, so I would always pray, "Jesus, on my day of delivery I want You to be the doctor to deliver me." The day before my due date, my daughter and I went to shop for the baby at The Galleria Mall. My water broke just as I pulled into the parking garage. Right away, I pulled out of the parking garage, paged my husband, and went to the hospital where I was scheduled to have the baby. When I arrived, they prepared me for delivery. The pain felt unbearable in the delivery room, so I kept asking the nurses for an epidural. They kept telling me to wait. While I was waiting I looked up, and Jesus was standing right below the TV.

I asked with surprise, "You here?" He said to me, "But of course, you asked me to be here." Right after that, the nurse came and gave me the epidural. I was relieved and I feel asleep—I am not sure for how long. When I woke up, I immediately remembered Jesus being there. I looked up, and He was still standing there.

I felt guilty. It was like a friend coming to visit you, and you ignored them and went to sleep. In this case, it was not just a friend; it was The King of Glory, the Creator and Ruler of the whole world. He had left His many important duties to come be with me in the delivery room—and I fell asleep on Him. Again, I was shocked and said, "You still here?" and He replied, "I will be here as long as you need me."

The doctors and nurses came in right after that conversation and said I was ready to have the baby. They told me to push. I pushed as hard as I could and nothing happened. I could still see Jesus looking over the shoulders of the doctors and nurses, observing everything that was happening—but He did not move. After a while—I'm not sure how much time had passed—He took a couple of steps forward, pointed at me, made eye contact, and said, "Now push." When He said that, both my body and the baby's immediately responded to His words, and the baby came into the world.

I have not viewed prayer the same way since that day. God hears our prayers and answers them the best way He sees fit, and in His own timing. I believe there was an ordained time for the baby to come into the world, and the LORD was not going to make it a moment sooner. He was going to be with me throughout the process, but He was not going to change the ordained delivery time of 1:21pm February 2, 1993.

Prayer works! Jesus came into that delivery room because I invited Him, to keep away any plans that the enemy may have had for my baby and me that day. God is good!

> *In prayer, we can come to God*
> *anytime, anywhere,*
> *and expect to receive an answer.*

When we pray over a situation, the ability of God takes over. God can do anything, anywhere, with anybody. He has control over all situations and circumstances. In prayer, we are finding out the will of God by communicating with Him, getting His plan, and asking Him for the grace to carry out His will.

This prayer book will give you powerful scriptures from the Bible and share how to apply them effectively. When we pray the Word of God, we are praying His will, and reminding Him of His promise. *"He who promised is faithful."*—*Hebrews 10:23.* Prayer exposes the secret behind the battle. In addition, it can change the trajectory of your life. Prayer helps you enter new levels, new dimensions, new favor, new breakthroughs, and new testimonies.

Review the table of contents of the book to find your area of need. Each chapter has prayer points to arm you with the powerful Word of the Living God. Following these prayer points are typical prayers that I pray. These sample prayers are weapons of warfare and blessings—use them as such. Allow them to inspire your own prayers. Sharpen them to be powerful and effective in your personal situation by personalizing the content as needed. Go to battle in prayer. Seek the answers God has for you. The power of praying the Word of God will change the situation for the better.

Section 1

KNOWING MY PLACE IN THE KINGDOM OF GOD

Chapter 1

WHAT IS PRAYER?

J esus had very much to teach about prayer. He spent a great deal of time in prayer. He refers to prayer in His teachings forty-two times, and the gospels record Him personally praying twenty-eight times. Several times, the Word of God tells us, *"...and He went up to the mountain to pray"—Matthew 14:23, Mark 6:46, Luke 6:12, and Luke 9:28.* He prayed in the wilderness, in the temple, in the Garden of Gethsemane, and on the cross. Prayer was a major part of the life of our Savior. Early on, the disciples came to Him and said, *"...Lord, teach us to pray..."—Luke 11:1.* They were amazed at the level of significance and the depth of meaning that prayer had for Jesus. His life was an eloquent expression of close communication with Almighty God.

Your prayer life will reflect your relationship with the LORD. The role of the Holy Spirit is to express the reality of Jesus Christ, and His power, in the life of the believer. Prayer accomplishes this; prayer helps you take control of your thoughts, actions, and reactions. Through prayer, the Holy Spirit will help you stay full of Him. When you are in line with Kingdom purpose, you are tied to Kingdom power.

What is in a prayer?

1. Adoration—*Psalms 150 and John 17:1-5*
2. Confession—*Psalms 51*
3. Thanksgiving—*Psalms 136 and Philippians 4:6*
4. Supplication (Intercession and Petition)—*John 17:6-26*

It is impossible to know God or please Him without believing and trusting in the fact that He hears and answers prayers.

In prayer we display our confidence in God's greatness, His ability, His love and His goodness—*Psalms 28*.

Prayer is talking to God about what is going on in your world and using His word, His Truth, as a weapon to bring a situation into agreement with Heaven. Your prayers are commands and decrees—they are mandates and instructions designed to create and change your world for the better.

Prayer is a place of refuge and strength. It is a place to use our faith to receive what we know God has for us and desires to give us—*2 Chronicles 7:14*. Prayer may not stop weapons from forming; but prayer will stop them from prospering. Prayer will encourage, protect, defend, support, and provide for you. It will not let you feel that you are alone—*Psalms 46:1*.

"I would have despaired unless I had believed that I would see the goodness of the Lord *In the land of the living."—Psalms 27:13 NASB.* You can depend upon God who said, *"I will never leave you nor forsake you"—Deuteronomy 31:6 and Hebrews 13:5.*

Do not let life merely happen to you. With prayer, you can break words against you, including hexes, spells, ill wishes, and curses. Be actively involved in facilitating, designing, constructing and engineering your life through the power of prayer.

Be specific in your prayer requests. Being specific ignites and awakens our faith and expectations. When you are specific in your requests, you will be clear in the answers you are expecting.

Prayer works only when we actually pray! We should pray when we feel like it and even more when we do not. This is usually when there is warfare going on in the spiritual realm. This is when we need to be handing the battle over to God in prayer, as well as getting instructions on what to do. If you will pray, God will answer. *"That is why I tell you, whatever you ask for in prayer, believe that you have received it and it will be yours."—Mark 11:24.*

In prayer, our heart must be hopeful; our expectations must be high; our soul open to God's direction and guidance; and our faith must be relentless—because He is faithful. *"Let us hold fast the profession of our faith without wavering; (for he is faithful that promised)."* —*Hebrews 10:23.*

The devil is not interested in your health, money, relationships, family, career or ministry. Let me tell you what I

> *When you are specific in your requests, you will be clear in the answers you are expecting.*

believe he is after—it is your faith. He knows without faith you cannot please God. The devil knows that anything that is not of faith is sin. He knows you are supposed to walk by faith, and not by sight. In addition, he knows that it takes faith for you to get your breakthrough, miracle, or have your own testimony. Whatever you do as a believer, do not let go of your faith. Jesus was always impressed with faith, and He said, *"According to your faith be it unto you."*—*Matthew 9:29.* In other words, your faith is what will produce your miracle.

Praying early causes your day to start with power and end with blessings. Start your day declaring the Word of God. The first words out of my mouth when I wake up in the morning, just as I am putting my feet on the ground are, *"This is the day which the LORD has made; I will rejoice and be glad in it."*—*Psalms 118:24.* I am declaring that God made this day, so nothing will tamper with my rejoicing and gladness, because the owner of this day is my source and resource. Prayers are spiritual incubators; they are pregnant with power, waiting for the ideal circumstance for manifestation. God hears every prayer. When a prayer is released, the spirit realm takes it as a command, an instruction, to carry out a task. Challenge yourself to spend more time in prayer, because God answers prayer. *"O thou that hearest prayer."*—*Psalms 65:2.*

In prayer, we can believe the unbelievable, obtain the inconceivable, reach the unimaginable and have the inexplicable. Prayer gives us the priceless gift of peace. *"Be careful for nothing; but in everything by prayer and supplication with thanksgiving let your requests be made known unto God, And the peace of God, which passeth all understanding, shall keep your hearts and minds through Christ Jesus."*—*Philippians 4:6-7.* We can measure our prayer life and dependence upon God by noting peace or lack of peace in our hearts. In all things, we are to seek the LORD and His continued presence. Peace will surely be our gain. *"Thou wilt keep him in perfect peace, whose mind is stayed on thee: because he trusteth in thee."—Isaiah 26:3.* I love and appreciate peace, so if I have to turn situations over to God in prayer, to have peace, that is exactly what I am going to do. It is impossible to know God or please Him without believing and trusting in the fact that He hears and answers prayer.

Prayer is acknowledging who God is. He responds to prayers in His Son's name. *"And whatsoever ye shall ask in my name, that will I do, that the Father may be glorified in the Son."—John 14:13.*

Chapter 2

TO KNOW GOD

E verything we go through brings us to where God wants us. When the world seems most out of control, God steps in to let us know that He is still in control and keeping watch over us. Often, it is only as we look back that we see the hand of God working through the affairs of life.

"He increased His people greatly, And made them stronger than their enemies. He turned their heart to hate His people, to deal craftily with His servants."—Psalms 105:24-25.

Anytime God removes protection and exposes us to the enemy, it is because He has made us stronger and has increased us. God has no difficulty defeating the devil. He has chosen to defeat the enemy with us and through us.

"You are my battle-ax and weapons of war: For with you I will break the nation in pieces."—Jeremiah 51:20 NKJV.

When Jesus died on the cross, He defeated Satan and his entire kingdom. *"For this purpose the Son of God was manifested, that he might destroy the works of the devil."—1 John 3:8 NKJV.* We are now called to enforce the victory that Jesus gained for us on the cross. *"So Jesus said to them again, "As the Father has sent Me, I also send you."—John 20:21 NKJV.*

The enemy hates us. God equips us to increase and be empowered to overcome the wicked one. Everyone is born for battle and conquest—to take territory for the King of Kings and to impact people for Him. David lost the battle with his eyes, which opened the door for him to lose the battle over his heart. He was not in the battle for which he was born. David was born to establish Israel to triumph in victory. Everyone is born for something—a place of victory and triumph, But when we turn away from our assigned battles, we face the battle we are not equipped for. Every one of us trained for some purpose. None of us has it all, but we have all been trained. We are equipped and prepared to be ready for conquest. When we are in the right battle, we bring about a shift—we change the atmosphere in our neighborhood, community and in government. Every one of us was born for something, but when we lose track of that purpose, we undergo battles we are not ready for—we become exposed to attacks we are not equipped to fight.

"...and this is the victory that overcomes the world..."—*1 John 5:4.* God has given us dominion. He is our Commander-in-Chief. We fight in the battles of the LORD, we are His battle-axe and weapons of war and our weapons are not carnal but spiritual.

Every warrior goes to battle with weapons of warfare that are trusted, effective and reliable. No warrior ever goes to battle without his weapon—there must be something with which the warrior hopes to fight.

When God says that you are His battle-axe, He is saying you are His weapon of warfare. He intends to fight battles through you. A battle-axe is anything in the hand of the warrior that is capable of bringing down the enemy. Therefore, God is saying with you in His hands, He will bring down the enemy. *"And the God of peace shall bruise Satan under your feet shortly."*—*Romans 16:20.*

Think about Moses when he went to Egypt to bring out the children of Israel. God told him, *"I have made you a god unto Pharaoh..."*—*Exodus 7:1.* This would mean that whatever God would have done by Himself to Pharaoh, He would do through Moses. Pharaoh did not see God, but he saw God's power working through Moses. As children of God, others will see the power of God working through us.

God controls our circumstances. The LORD allows difficulty in our lives. He wants to teach us dependence on Him to stretch us and make us stronger for winning spiritual, mental, and emotional battles.

We have what we need to defeat the enemy because of what Jesus did. He has already equipped us to win this battle. A good axe is strong, swift, powerful, sharp, and capable. Any time you are under attack, know that the enemy is trying to scare you to make you afraid, nervous, and anxious. The enemy just makes a lot of noise. *"...the devil walks about like a roaring lion, seeking whom he may devour."—1 Peter 5:8.*

The enemy's strategy is to intimidate you and distract you from hearing God. When you are fearful and nervous, it is hard to hear from God. When you don't hear from God, you cannot get instructions and strategies on what to do to win the battle.

God has positioned you for strength in the day of battle. *"For thou hast girded me with strength to battle."—II Samuel 22:40 NKJV.* Any time the LORD takes us into a battle, He knows He has thoroughly equipped us for victory.

When you are fearful and anxious, you can forget what God has done, who He is, and what He can do.

Everyone is born for something— a place of victory and triumph

When you face a battle, look back at what God has shown you and taught you. You will realize that God has fully equipped you to overcome and win this battle. As the scripture says, *"I will remember the works of the LORD; Surely I will remember your wonders of old. I will also meditate on all your work, and talk of your deeds."—Psalms 77:11-12 NKJV.*

We pray for the problem to go away when what we need is not always for the problem to go away, but for a Word, a promise from God, a prophetic word, or a Rhema word.

Sometimes the LORD does not want to do something for me because He has already done His work in me. Now He wants to do something through me—to use me. To win this battle, I must arm myself with the Word—the Sword of the Spirit. That is when you open your mouth and decree the word of God. Fight for your life, family, relationship, health, and finances with the word of God, with worship and with prayer.

There are some battles that God does not want you to fight, because He wants to do it for you. Our job is to just stand and see the salvation of the LORD, *"Be still and know that I am God."— Psalms 46:10 NKJV. "And he said, "...King Jehoshaphat! Thus says the LORD to you: 'Do not be afraid nor dismayed because of this great multitude, for the battle is not yours, but God's."—2 Chronicles 20:15 NKJV.*

Other times, you are to get actively involved in the warfare, change positions, and co-labor with God. Arm yourself with the Word of the LORD. Put it in your mouth, memorize it, learn to pray it, and learn to worship. When Moses worshipped with arms lifted high, his people were winning, but when his arms got tired and dropped, they would start losing. God is trying to raise an army that doesn't just need to be delivered, but knows how to be a deliverer. He is trying to raise an army that doesn't just need to be rescued, but knows how to be a rescuer.

God is always with us. The LORD promises to be with us at all times, although we may not feel His presence and loving care. If you have received Jesus Christ as your personal Savior, His Spirit lives within you. Who shall separate us from the love of Christ? Shall tribulation, or distress, or persecution, or famine, or nakedness, or peril, or sword? As it is written:

"For Your sake we are killed all day long; We are accounted as sheep for the slaughter." Yet in all these things we are more than conquerors through Him who loved us. For I am persuaded that neither death nor life, nor angels nor principalities nor powers, nor things present nor things to come, nor height nor depth, nor any other created thing, shall be able to separate us from the love of God which is in Christ Jesus our Lord."—Romans 8:35-39 NKJV, Psalms 23, and Matthew 18:19-20. Those who reject Jesus do not have this promise. God loves us with an eternal love.

God governs our lives, but that does not mean our existence will be trouble-free. For example, one Iranian man spent 12 years in prison for refusing to deny His faith in Jesus Christ.

Do you ever feel that life is one challenge after another? The truth is that hardship comes to everyone sometimes. If you have been facing an illness, relationship problems–things we all encounter, ask the LORD to give you a Word. Ask Him to give you a promise that you can specifically use against that problem. We have confidence in troubled times when we hold onto a Word from God.

When unexpected tragedy or hardship comes your way, remember that God is still in control. Your Heavenly Father provides for your needs in His timing. Knowing God is the key to placing your full trust in Him and having confidence in every circumstance.

Prayer Points—Open your mouth and pray

"That I may know him, and the power of his resurrection, and the fellowship of his sufferings, being made conformable unto his death."—Philippians 3:10 NKJV.

Father, give me the grace to know You, to know who You are in a personal way. Give me a revelation of who You are. LORD, reveal Your power in my life, manifest Your love. You are a merciful God; show me Your mercy in a new way, in Jesus' name.

Almighty God, show me the power of Your resurrection and reveal that power in my life. Let the power of Your resurrection manifest in all that concerns me, in the name of Jesus. Father, resurrect my relationships and resurrect my mind. King of kings, resurrect my wealth. My LORD and my God, today may You resurrect my virtues and glory that the enemy has buried. LORD, resurrect them all in the mighty name of Jesus.

"But if anyone loves God, this one is known by Him."
—1 Corinthians 8:3 NKJV.

Make a declaration of your love for God today. Father, I love You. Lord Jesus, I love You. Holy Spirit, I love You. LORD, know me. Father, know me in a new way and purify my heart with Your presence.

LORD, give me anointed ideas and lead me to new path of blessings, in Jesus' name.

LORD, starting this month I want to know You like I have never known You. Let this month be the month I start to hear You more, feel You more, and love You more.

Almighty God, let this season be the one where I start to experience Your love in a new way, in the name of Jesus.

"Then I will give them a heart to know Me, that I am the LORD; and they shall be My people, and I will be their God, for they shall return to Me with their whole heart."—Jeremiah 24:7 NKJV.

✟ Knowing God starts from the heart. LORD, give me a heart to know You, that You are the LORD, a heart that seeks You, give me a heart that is sold out to You. LORD, give me Your heart.

✟ Father, make me one of Your people, and I ask You to become my God.

✟ Father, bring me back to You. Help me to return to You. Help me to return with my whole heart, in the name of Jesus.

✟ Pray that all inherited limitations to obtaining intimacy with God depart from your life, in the name of Jesus.

✟ I command every spiritual contamination in my life to receive spiritual healing, by the blood of Jesus. LORD, drain out all evil deposits from my life.

"That the God of our Lord Jesus Christ, the Father of glory, may give to you the spirit of wisdom and revelation in the knowledge of Him."—Ephesians 1:17 NKJV.

It takes wisdom to know God and to serve Him. It takes wisdom to fear God.

✟ Father, I receive Your most awesome gifts of the spirit of wisdom and of revelation knowledge of You. I seek those gifts with all my heart, mind, and soul, and thank You for them in the name of Jesus.

✟ Father, open the floodgates of Heaven and open my heart, mind, and soul to receive all that You have for me.

"The fear of the LORD is the beginning of wisdom: a good understanding have all they that do his commandments: his praise endureth for ever."—Psalms 111:10 NKJV.

✠ Pray for wisdom from Heaven above, wisdom to fear and adore God for who He is. *LORD*, grant me the Spirit of revelation in the knowledge of Christ.

"That Christ may dwell in your hearts through faith; that you, being rooted and grounded in love."—Ephesians 3:17 NKJV.

✠ Almighty God, by faith, come and dwell in my heart. *LORD*, bless me with the faith to trust in Your love, bless me with faith that will believe You and Your love for me. Give me faith for my miracle, in the name of Jesus.

✠ From today, I shall be rooted and grounded in Your love, in the name of Jesus. I shall be rooted and grounded in Your mercy and goodness, in Jesus' name.

✠ Almighty God, in this season, let the spirit of favor fall upon me, and upon all that I do, in the name of Jesus.

"I will instruct you and teach you in the way you should go; I will guide you with My eye."—Psalms 32:8 NKJV.

✠ *LORD*, instruct me and teach me in the way I should go. Father God, be the one leading me in all areas. Teach me a new thing this season. Help me to get Your revelation about what You have been trying to say to me in the name of Jesus.

✠ Father, guide me with Your eyes, in the name of Jesus.

"Serve the LORD with gladness; Come before His presence with singing. Know that the LORD, He is God; It is He who has made us, and not we ourselves; We are His people and the sheep of His pasture."—Psalms 100:2-3 NKJV.

✠ *LORD*, I will serve You with gladness. Anything stealing my gladness must end today, in Jesus' name. The joy of the *LORD* shall be my strength, in the name of Jesus.

✝ I shall come to the presence of God with singing; there shall be songs of praise in my mouth all the days of my life, in the name of Jesus.

✝ *LORD*, You made me. I am Yours—the sheep of Your pasture. Therefore, *LORD*, take care of me as Your sheep.

✝ Father, today keep me close to You and release Your angels to police my life for the rest of my life. My intimacy with God shall frustrate, disappoint, and disapprove every enemy's plans against me, in Jesus' name.

From Dr. Pat: I pray for you, in the name of Jesus. I bind all anti-breakthrough, anti-prosperity, and anti-miracle forces working against your destiny, in the name of Jesus.

Chapter 3

MY HOPE IS IN GOD

God delights in those who place their hope in Him. In Him, we find hope that does not fail. Placing your hope on people can disappoint, but placing your hope in God is wisdom. Hope in God, is hope not based upon circumstances, but absolute faith in Him and His promises.

Hope comes from trusting Christ. Jairus' case looked hopeless. He may have been worried, afraid, and without hope, but Jesus' words to Jairus in the midst of crisis, speaks to us as well. *"As soon as Jesus heard the word that was spoken, He said to the ruler of the synagogue, 'Do not be afraid; only believe."—Mark 5:36 NKJV.* Whenever you face difficulties, look for a word from God—look for a promise or a special word for that situation. That divine promise is going to remove fear and take away anxiety. The word of God is going to silence the noise of the enemy and produce hope in you that all is well.

Look to Jesus the next time you feel hopeless and afraid. Jesus is the solution to all situations. He is the source of all hope and promise. Hope comes from remembering all that God has done, and is able to do, for us.

Hope grows as we depend on God in the difficult times. Hope grows as we learn all that God has planned for us, and that hope gives us excitement about the promise of the future. God's love fills our lives and gives us the ability to rest in Him. No matter what the issue looks like, hope springs up. A situation may look dark right now, and it may look like there is no way out. You may not know how you are going to make it from one day to the other, and a situation may really look hopeless, dead, and just plain out of control. The Word of God says that the light is going to shine again, and it will shine brighter than you have ever seen.

"Then spoke Jesus again to them, saying, I am the light of the world: he that follows me shall not walk in darkness, but shall have the light of life."—John 8:12 NKJV. While trouble can bring a sense of despair, we can be confident that God is behind the scenes, manipulating and controlling the situation for our good and His glory.

I heard an interesting story recently.

A king, who did not believe in the goodness of God, had a slave who, in all circumstances would always say, "My king, do not be discouraged, because everything God does is perfect. He makes no mistakes!"

One day they went hunting and a wild animal attacked the king. His slave managed to kill the animal, but could not prevent his majesty from losing a finger. Furious and without showing his gratitude for being saved, the nobleman asked, "Is God good? If He was good, I would not have been attacked and lost my finger."

The slave replied, "My king, despite all these things, I can only tell you that God is good, and He knows why these things happened. What God does is perfect. He is never wrong!"

Outraged by the response, the king ordered the arrest of his slave. Later, the King left for another hunt, this time alone. Savages who engaged in human sacrifices captured him. On the altar and ready to sacrifice the nobleman, the savages discovered that their victim did not have one of his fingers. According to them, only a whole person with all of their parts intact could qualify as an offering to their gods. Missing a finger, the king was an abominable sacrifice for their gods so they released him. Upon his return to the palace, the King authorized the release of his slave. He received the slave affectionately and said, "My dear, God was really good to me! I was almost killed by the wild men, but for lack of a single finger, I was let go! I have a question though. If God is so good, why did He allow me to put you in jail?"

The slave answered, "My King, if I had gone with you on this hunt, I would have been sacrificed instead, because I have no missing finger. Remember everything God does is perfect. He is never wrong. He made you keep me in jail so I would not be with you on the hunt."

Often we complain about life, and negative things that happen to us, because we forget that nothing is random and that everything has a purpose.

When light shows up, darkness has to give way, it has to leave, so a situation that looks dark right now is going to change as you turn it over to Jesus. Your pain will determine your passion. Your situation will never determine your revelation. Your hope is firm and fixed on God and you know that He cannot fail! As long as you have an expectation, God will not let it be cut off. Your situation is about to change. The hard times are about to change, if you will trust God. The pain in your life will bring you to a new place—a great place. The LORD is not far from us when we call upon Him. He will answer. He has answers for all your challenges. Just *"cast these burdens on Him, He will sustain you, uphold you and keep you."*—Psalms 55:22. From Genesis to Revelation, God reveals His unconditional love and concern for His people. As you pray about hope today, receive your promises from God for you. Allow the promises of God to encourage, guide, and transform your life.

Prayer Points—Open your mouth and pray

✝ Almighty God, we release all our burdens to You. We thank You for keeping us. LORD, help us to overcome all stress and pain, in Jesus' name.
✝ Let every pain in our lives bring us passion that will birth purpose and greatness, in the name of Jesus.

The difference between significant and insignificant is an enemy. The difference between important and unimportant is an

adversary. The enemy you overcome determines the promotion and success you receive.

✞ Father, give me the enablement to overcome and be promoted. I shall overcome all hopelessness in my situation, in the name of Jesus.

✞ I pray for anointing to be recognized for good. LORD, I thank You for announcing and advertising me, in this season, in the name of Jesus.

One bad day can create a domino effect of bad days and years. Reject a bad day that can produce a ripple of bad experiences. One good day can birth many good days and good years. Even the rest of your life can become very good—it starts with the first good day.

✞ LORD, thank You for a good day that will change everything for the better in my life. Thank You for that good day that will produce my testimony, in Jesus' name.

"Rejoice in hope, be patient in tribulation, be constant in prayer."—Romans 12:12.

Sometimes life catches you by surprise and you feel unequipped to handle what it brings you, but every bit of life you've lived before that moment equips you to live through it.

✞ Though I have received blow after blow, from now on, every one of them will be reversed and become a stepping-stone. LORD, let every adversity bring achievement and success to my life, for all things are destined to work together for my good.

> *Allow the promises of God to encourage, guide, and transform your life.*

✞ Almighty God, I celebrate my hope in You. Let me not be put to shame. Grant me patience in all tribulations, and help me to be constant in prayer. Give me the grace to hope in Your goodness and not give up on prayer and Your promise, in the name of Jesus.

✢ *LORD*, cut down every power that is challenging our hope and glory, in Jesus' name.

✢ Holy Ghost, fill us, that we might bring forth glory to God, in the name of Jesus.

✢ Let my spirit-man become divine fire, be ignited for expectation, and be fired up in hope and faith in God's goodness, in the name of Jesus.

"May the God of hope fill you with all joy and peace in believing, so that by the power of the Holy Spirit you may abound in—hope."—Romans 15:13 ESV.

✢ God of hope, fill me with joy and peace in believing, so that by the power of the Holy Spirit I may abound in hope. *LORD*, fill me with everything that You are, so my hope may remain in You, in the name of Jesus.

"Though he slay me, I will hope in him; yet I will argue my ways to his face."—Job 13:15 NIV.

✢ *LORD*, no matter what it looks like, I shall continue to hold on to my hope in You, for I know You are a good God, and You have good plans for my life.

"Return to your fortress, O prisoners of hope; even now I announce that I will restore twice as much to you"— Zechariah 9:12 NIV.

✢ I am arrested by my hope in God, so I can return to my fortress. God shall restore to me double for all my trouble, in the name of Jesus. I have unfailing hope and confidence in God, and I shall possess double blessings in all areas of life, in the mighty name of Jesus.

Chapter 4

O LORD, INTERCEDE FOR ME

S ometimes when we are going through a hard time, we need
prayer the most. The Holy Spirit intercedes on our behalf when
we find it difficult and need help praying about the situation.

> *"Likewise the Spirit also helps in our weaknesses. For we do
> not know what we should pray for as we ought, but the Spirit
> Himself makes intercession for us with groanings which
> cannot be uttered." — Romans 8:26 NKJV.*

> *"He made him draw honey from the rock and oil from the
> flinty rock." — Deuteronomy 32:13 NKJV.*

We know that a stone cannot produce oil; neither can honey come
out of a rock. These are impossible things. What the Bible is saying is
that no matter how rough the situation is, no matter how terrible the
economy is, the LORD God of Heaven and Earth is able to squeeze
out your miracle for you.

Prayer Points — Open your mouth and pray

✟ Holy Spirit of God, help me overcome my weakness, be
strong in my life where I am weak, when I don't know what
to pray or how to pray. Intercede for me when I don't pray,
Holy Spirit, stand in the gap for me, mediate on my behalf,
intervene for me in the spiritual realm, in the name of Jesus.

"For He who is mighty has done great things for me."—
Luke 1:9 NKJV.

✛ Almighty God, You are the same yes-terday, today, and forever. As You did great things for

> After today, your life will receive the supernatural touch of God, in the name of Jesus.

Elizabeth, do something great in my life. Father, do a great thing in my situation, do a great thing in my marriage. Thank You, LORD, for doing great things in the lives of my children. Today, my King, do something great in my finances. LORD, in all areas of my life, wherever I need help, move for me and do a great thing, in the name of Jesus.

✛ Pray and ask the LORD to use this prayer to reveal and release His power and glory to you today.

It takes grace to be successful.

✛ I receive the grace to move up in life. LORD, grant me the grace that will move me to the next level of glory, grant me the grace I need to get promotion. I receive the grace to be selected for compensation, reward, inheritance and great blessings, in the name of Jesus.

✛ LORD deliver me from bondages that I have gotten used to, all the things that are less than God's best for my life that I've accepted; the sickness, poverty, depression, constant demonic attack. Father, deliver me from them. I am set free from loneliness, shame, reproach, and abandonment, in the name of Jesus.

✛ Almighty God, put into my life the gift that will elevate my life. I receive the talent that will promote me. LORD, grant me the abilities that will open mighty doors of opportunities for me. I pray that the LORD will maximize my potential from this day forth, in the name of Jesus.

✛ In the evil world, they release curses on people just because. *"Like a fluttering sparrow or a darting swallow, an undeserved curse does not come to rest."* —*Proverb 26:2 NIV.* I pray that no curse will manifest in my life. No curse on me released by a power, person, or issue will prevail, in the name of Jesus.

"The LORD thy God turned the curse into a blessing unto thee, because the LORD thy God loved thee."
—Deuteronomy 23:5.

✝ Father God, as You turned Balaam's curse into blessings for the children of Israel, turn all the enemies' curses into blessings in my life, in the name of Jesus.

✝ Father, after today's prayer, let life become easier for me, may it be easier for me to love, easier to succeed, easier to get along with people, easier to study and understand the Word of God. *LORD*, let it be easier to pray and spend time with You. Father, let it be easier for me to be accepted, and have favor with God and men, in the name of Jesus.

✝ Father God, help me to achieve good success in all areas of life. What no one thought I could achieve, grant me the grace to exceed them. *LORD*, empower me to exceed the expectations of those who have counted me out, in the name of Jesus.

Let the power and goodness of God help you accomplish what others have not been able to achieve. What has taken others a lifetime to achieve, let the grace of God help you achieve it in record time, in the name of Jesus.

✝ Pray and ask the *LORD* for the key to good success, so that everywhere you go, the door of good success will be open unto you. Both professionally and personally, receive the key to open the door of great success, in the name of Jesus. It is your turn to be blessed and your turn for testimonies. Now is your season for miracles, in the mighty name of Jesus. No more delay, no more hindrances, no more sabotage. You are moving forward into the great things you know God has for you, in Jesus' name.

✟ Almighty God, send the blood of Jesus today, and destroy every evil power pulling down my progress, in the name of Jesus.

"Therefore He is also able to save to the uttermost those who come to God through Him, since He always lives to make intercession for them."—Hebrews 7:25 NKJV.

✟ Lord Jesus, thank You for bringing us to God through Your sacrifice, thank You for saving us, we are thankful that You were raised on the third day, and now You live to make intercession for all believers. May Your intercession manifest in all areas of my life. Thank You, Jesus.
✟ From Dr. Pat: After today, your life will receive the supernatural touch of God, in the name of Jesus.

Chapter 5

HOW TO BECOME A
BORN AGAIN CHRISTIAN

W hat is the prayer of salvation? Many people ask, "Is there a prayer I can pray that will guarantee my salvation?" Uttering certain words or reciting words from some prayer is not a "Hocus Pocus" that produces salvation. Salvation is not received by just reciting a prayer or uttering certain words.

The biblical method of salvation is faith in Jesus Christ. The Bible tells us, *"For God so loved the world that he gave his one and only Son, that whoever believes in him shall not perish but have eternal life."—John 3:16.* Salvation is gained by faith *(Ephesians 2:8)*, by receiving Jesus as Savior *(John 1:12)*, and by fully trusting Jesus alone *(John 14:6; Acts 4:12)*.

The biblical message of salvation is simple, clear, and amazing at the same time.

We have all committed sin against God *(Romans 3:23)*. Other than Jesus Christ, there is no one who has lived an entire life without sinning *(Ecclesiastes 7:20)*. Because of our sin, we have earned judgment from God *(Romans 6:23)*, and that judgment is physical death followed by spiritual death.

There is nothing we can do, on our own, to make ourselves right with God. We deserve punishment because of our sin. Because of His love for us, God became a human being in the person of Jesus Christ. Jesus lived a perfect life and always taught the truth. Jesus took the burden and judgment of sin on Himself, and He died in our place *(2 Corinthians 5:21)*. Jesus was then resurrected *(1 Corinthians 15)*, proving that His payment for sin was sufficient and that He had overcome sin and death. Because of Jesus' sacrifice, God offers us salvation as a gift. God calls us all to change our minds about Jesus *(Acts 17:30)* and to receive Him as the full payment of our sins *(1 John 2:2)*. Salvation is gained by receiving the gift God offers us and by praying a prayer to ask Jesus into our lives.

If you understand the gospel and believe it to be true, it is good and appropriate to express that faith to God in prayer. Communicating with God through prayer can be a way to progress from asking Jesus into your life, to fully trusting in Him as Savior. Pray placing your faith in Jesus alone for salvation.

Do not base your salvation on having said a prayer alone. Reciting a prayer cannot save you if you lack understanding of Jesus and faith in Jesus as Savior and Lord! If you want to receive the salvation that is available through Jesus, place your faith in Him based on what He has done for you. Fully trust His death as the sufficient sacrifice for your sins.

> *Completely rely on Him alone as your Savior, and then pray to open the door of your heart to invite Jesus into your life.*

Completely rely on Him alone as your Savior, and then pray to open the door of your heart to invite Jesus into your life. Offer praise to God for His love and sacrifice. Thank Jesus for dying for your sins and providing salvation for you.

If you are ready to make a personal commitment to follow Christ, all you have to do is reach out to Him now in prayer. He is listening and waiting to come into your heart and help you live a better life. Will you invite Him in now?

"That if thou shalt confess with thy mouth the Lord Jesus, and shalt believe in thine heart that God hath raised him from the dead, thou shalt be saved. For with the heart man believeth unto righteousness; and with the mouth confession is made unto salvation." —Romans 10:9-10.

Prayer Points—Open your mouth and pray

If you want to pray and receive Christ as your Savior, you can use this simple prayer as a guide:

Dear God in Heaven, I come to You in the name of Jesus. I acknowledge to You that I am a sinner, and I am sorry for my sins and the life that I have lived. I need Your forgiveness. I confess my sins before You this day. I denounce Satan and all his works. I confess Jesus as the Lord of my life. Thank You for saving me. I believe with my heart and I confess with my mouth that You raised Jesus from death to life. As of now, I am saved. Write my name in the Lamb's book of life.

I believe that Your only begotten Son Jesus Christ shed His precious blood on the cross at Calvary and died for my sins, and I am now willing to turn from my sin.

I confess Jesus as the Lord of my soul. With my heart, I believe that God raised Jesus from the dead. I accept Jesus Christ as my own personal Savior and according to His Word, right now I am saved.

I ask You to take control of my life. I give it to You. Help me to live every day in a way that pleases You. I love You, LORD, and I thank You that I will spend all eternity with You.

Thank You Jesus, for Your unlimited grace which has saved me from my sins. I thank You Jesus that Your grace never leads to license—it always leads to repentance. Lord Jesus change my life so that I may bring glory and honor to You alone, and not to myself.

Thank You Jesus, for dying for me and giving me eternal life.

Amen.

Strategic Ways To Pray for Salvation for Others

Unbelief cripples many when they pray for salvation of the lost. Perhaps it's because they've prayed and waited so long that they are no longer convinced God will really save those for whom they pray.

This unbelief renders our prayers powerless. If we don't believe God will answer our prayers, we will not pray with power, authority, consistency, and diligence. We may sporadically ask Him, but we certainly will not persevere.

Our purpose as a generation is to bring in the greatest harvest of souls the world has ever seen. Our purpose is to do the will of God on Earth, as it is in Heaven. *"For David, after he had served the purpose of God in his own generation, fell asleep" Acts 13:36—NASB.*

To accomplish that purpose, we must do Kingdom work. Much of it involves strategic prayers to release our loved ones from Satan's lies.

The Bible tells us, *"The god of this world has blinded the minds of the unbelieving, that they might not see the light of the gospel of the glory of Christ, who is the image of God"—2 Corinthians 4:4 NASB.*

There is a covering over the minds of unbelievers that keep them from clearly seeing the light and truth of the gospel. Unbelievers will not understand the gospel until they have a divine revelation, because the veil prevents them from comprehending it.

Satan's goal is to hide the truth of the gospel in order to keep unbelievers in his grip. How does he accomplish this? Satan has an ability to dull the unbeliever's thinking where the gospel is concerned. He is a liar, specializing in making lies look like the truth because he comes in disguise. *"For Satan himself transforms himself into an angel of light."—2 Corinthians 11:14 NKJV.* The veil of pride causes most to reject Christ, whether from the works motivation of false religions or because most people don't want to give lordship of their lives to another.

How do we deal with the vision-altering force of pride inflicted upon us by Satan himself? The Bible identifies a solution for the pride problem and gives us key strategies for effectively praying for unbelievers.

"For though we walk in the flesh, we do not war according to the flesh. For the weapons of our warfare are not carnal but mighty in God for pulling down strongholds, casting down arguments and every high thing that exalts itself against the knowledge of God, bringing every thought into captivity to the obedience of Christ," —2 Cor. 10:3-5 NKJV.

"...Blessed are you, Simon Bar-Jonah, for flesh and blood has not revealed this to you, but my Father who is in heaven."—Matthew 16:17. We will never win people to Christ on an intellectual basis or through innovative methods alone. As the passage above notes, the Father reveals to a person that Jesus came to redeem—it requires revelation. Certainly, a continual barrage of nagging and harassing tactics won't bring them to the LORD.

Some wives believed it was their job to do everything in their power to 'make' their husbands become Christians, but by their manipulative scheming, they only succeeded in turning their husbands away from any interest in spiritual matters. Many wives have learned the hard way, that only the Holy Spirit can reveal to an individual the truth of who Jesus is.

"Wives, likewise, be submissive to your own husbands, that even if some do not obey the word, they, without a word, may be won by the conduct of their wives, when they observe your chaste conduct accompanied by fear." — 1 Peter 3:1-2 NKJV.

Sometimes we can talk people into a salvation prayer without a true revelation (unveiling), but there is usually no real change because there is no true repentance, which comes only from biblical revelation.

When we approach people on a human basis, especially if they feel we are pressuring them, we generally make things worse. The root of pride in them rises up and defends itself. If we attack this pride on a human level, we will only strengthen it.

We have weapons that are "divinely powerful." These God empowered weapons will work miracles.

GOD'S ARMOR FOR BREAKING HUMAN PRIDE

Paul E. Billheimer, a 20th-century authority on prayer and author of "Destined for the Throne" (Christian Literature Crusade), said his salvation resulted from spiritual warfare waged on his behalf. He explains: "My mother used these weapons on me. I was as hostile to God as any sinner. I was fighting with all my might. But the time came when it was easier to lay down my arms of rebellion than to continue my resistance. The pressure exerted upon me by the Holy Spirit became so powerful that I voluntarily sought relief by yielding my rebellious will. The wooing of divine love was so strong that of my own free will I fell into the arms of redeeming grace. I became a willing 'captive.' "

What are these weapons we use in our warfare?

All forms of prayer. This includes supplication, agreement with other Christians, travail, praying in the Spirit, binding and loosing— any biblical form of prayer. See *Ephesians 6:18*.

Chapter 6

THE POWER OF THE BLOOD OF JESUS

First, we found that Christ is our Passover. To be our Passover, He had to be a lamb—a male without blemish. He had to be kept and then killed, and then His blood had to be applied on the doorposts. If He is our Passover, all of that had to be done.

The high priest took that blood in the basin once a year on the Day of Atonement, walked inside the tabernacle, and sprinkled that blood seven times on the mercy seat. Jesus was the Lamb who died, but He was also the High Priest. This is why Jesus must be raised from the dead. Jesus, as the sacrifice, is not the total Savior—unless He is at the right hand of the Father pleading our case as our High Priest. There are three parts to the Gospel: death, burial, and resurrection. The resurrection was necessary because the High Priest, Jesus, had to be raised from the dead so He can be our Passover, and for Him to be our Passover the blood must be applied.

Christ presides as our High Priest. He comes before the Father as our Advocate to mediate on our behalf.

"Without the shedding of blood, there is no remission of sins."—Hebrews 9:22.

The blood of Jesus cleanses us from all sins. Jesus came to die for the sins of the world and His blood was shed to restore us to the Father. You can claim the cleansing power in His blood and God will open a new chapter in your life. Let the power in the blood cleanse and make you whole. The blood of Jesus, is one of the most powerful thing Jesus came to give us, to bring us victory. Take the blood from the body and you have nothing left but a corpse. Take the blood of Christ from the body of Christ and you have a lifeless faith instead of a living faith. God says clearly, *"For the life of the flesh is in the blood."*—*Leviticus 17:11.*

Judas the betrayer spoke of it as *"innocent blood"*—*Matthew 27:4*, and Peter called it *"the precious blood of Christ, as of a lamb without blemish and without spot"*—*1 Peter 1:9 NIV.* It is the cleansing blood in *1 John 1:7* and the washing blood in *Revelation 1:5*, stressing that it removes the guilt of our sins.

You can plead the blood of Jesus over any and everything: your spirit, soul, and body, your house, car, work, children, spouse, and business, as a form of protection or prevention all against evil.

I heard about a story of a woman in my church, who locked herself out of her house one day. She went to ask her next-door neighbor, a Locksmith, to come open the door with his general key. He tried the front door and it did not open. He tried the back door and it did not work. She murmured under her breath, "Lord why is this not working?" She said the Lord spoke to her, and said, "You have covered your house with the blood of Jesus, and it will not let any stranger in." It was then she prayed, *"Lord temporarily remove the blood so he can open the door."* The Locksmith was able to open the door after that prayer. My friends, there is power in the blood.

Blood is a living thing, and the blood of Jesus has the power to overcome anything that confronts you. However, there is a small condition. For you to plead the blood of Jesus and have it work for you, you must be a born again Christian, you must give your life to Jesus. Just pray this simple prayer and believe with your heart that Jesus will come in and change your life. Call out to Jesus, "Lord Jesus, forgive me of my sins, come into my life, and be my Lord and Savior. Today I surrender to You as my Redeemer. Write my name in the book of life that I belong to You. Thank You, Lord, for saving me by Your grace, to become a born again Christian." If you have just said this prayer for the first time, you must get into a Bible teaching church, read the word of God daily, and talk with God daily in prayer.

Prayer Points—Open your mouth and pray

✠ Almighty God arm us with the cleansing strength in the blood of Jesus Christ, that we may be forgiven every sin, in the name of Jesus.

Peace can be enjoyed but not without blood *"having made peace through the blood of His cross."—Colossians 1:20.*

✠ Father, give me peace in my walk with You, let me have the peace that Jesus died for me to possess, let my home be transformed with peace through the blood, grant me peace in my body by the blood, in Jesus' name.

✠ Mountain-moving power: this is the miracle of, "How did it happen?"—an inexplicable move of God that can manifest by the blood of Jesus. Pray for inexplicable miracles to manifest in your life by the blood of Jesus Christ.

✠ Wherever my name and pictures have been taken for evil, let the blood of Jesus nullify them.

✠ Every power of familiar spirits assigned to monitor me, to attack me, be destroyed, by the blood of Jesus.

✠ Blood of Jesus Christ changes a person, inside out. Blood of Jesus Christ, wash away everything in our lives that is not like Jesus.

✠ Blood of Jesus Christ, remove all stains of evil in our lives. Any area of our lives that is unclean, receive the cleansing power of the blood of Jesus Christ.

✠ I command everything in my body to receive divine recreation, and be made whole and healthy, in Jesus' name.

✠ You can plead the blood of Jesus over your journey, the road, the vehicle or aircraft, etc. If you are living or passing through a dangerous zone, you can draw a bloodline of protection, therefore making a boundary against any evil.

✠ Blood of Jesus, give me life, give me a fulfilled life, give me an abundant life.

> *Jesus came to die for the sins of the world and His blood was shed to restore us to the Father.*

Blood of Jesus, grant me a life that is full of Your life, in the name of Jesus.

The Blood is protection: *"... and when I see the blood, I will pass over you, and the plague shall not be upon you to destroy you, when I smite the land of Egypt."—Exodus 12:13.*

✟ I command the following to pass over my house and my life: Poverty, loneliness and rejection, sickness and disease, shame, joblessness, curses, death, failure, depression, oppression, sadness, hopelessness, recession, limitation, delayed blessings, reproach, discouragement, discontentment, worry, anxiety, abandonment, insecurity, disgrace, dishonor, humiliation and all demonic attacks. Blood of Jesus, make death pass over me. Blood of Jesus, do not permit sudden and untimely death to touch my family or me. All of these things must all pass over my life and my family's life, in Jesus' name.

"To Jesus the Mediator of the new covenant and to the blood of sprinkling that speaks better things than that of Abel."—Hebrews 12:24 NKJV.

✟ Blood of Jesus, speak better things into my life this year. Speak better things into my marriage, speak better things into my children, and speak better things into my finances. Blood of Jesus, speak better things into my health, and speak better things into my career. Blood of Jesus, speak better things into my family, in the name of Jesus.

✟ Blood of Jesus, arise and fight all of our battles. Remove every obstacle and opposition, in the name of Jesus.

✟ Blood of Jesus, chase poverty and lack out of our lives. We will not suffer financial shame, in the name of Jesus.

✟ I pray for our blessings to be rapid, and from expected and unexpected sources, God will bring our blessings.

The Blood: Sanctification: *"Wherefore Jesus also, that he might sanctify the people with his own blood, suffered without the gate."—Hebrews 13:12.*

After the blood has cleansed you, you now need to be sanctified. Pray to be sanctified and purified by the blood of Jesus.

- ✟ I receive the benefit of the suffering of Christ. I receive all that Jesus died for me to have, His riches, anointing, healing, authority, and blessings, in Jesus' name.
- ✟ Wherever my blessing is, be returned to me by the blood of Jesus.

Poison-destroying power: **Some people have been poisoned physically or spiritually. The blood of Jesus will neutralize such poison and flush it out of the system.**

- ✟ I command all my blessings confiscated by rulers of darkness to be released, by the power in the blood of Jesus.
- ✟ Decree life-giving power to revive anyone or anything that is dead. It could be marriage, finances, business, etc.
- ✟ Decree yoke-destroying power. Whenever you plead the blood of Jesus, people and things are set free from any kind of yoke repression, depression, burden, or bondage.
- ✟ I pray no evil power can stand the blood. Blood of Jesus, bring to an end all demonic activities in my life and the life of my loved ones, in the name of Jesus.

The blood gives us victory: *"And they overcame him (Satan) by the blood of the Lamb, and by the word of their testimony ..."—Revelation 12:11.*

- ✟ Decree deliverance: When you call the blood of Jesus into operation, it causes the enemy to flee, because it contains the life of God. It sets people free from bondage.

✞ Decree healing: It can heal all forms of infirmity. When you plead the blood of Jesus, things begin to happen. It releases the healing power in His stripes.

Chapter 7

HOLY SPIRIT, OUR DIVINE HELPER

The Holy Spirit is our teacher and enables us to know the things of God.

We should be overjoyed to learn what great provision God has made for us through the ministry of His Holy Spirit. He is God's perpetual, indwelling gift to you. He should not be ignored—we should yield to Him. The Holy Spirit is the agent of our prayers. He is the one that moves our prayers by His power back to the Father through Christ.

The biblical answer to the question of, "Who is the Holy Spirit?" is threefold. First, the Holy Spirit is divine. Second, the Holy Spirit is a unique person of the Godhead. Third, the Holy Spirit has a unique role in the Godhead.

He intercedes for us. Our prayers wouldn't have a chance of reaching God or of being effective without the Holy Spirit's intercession. He makes our prayers acceptable to God. As Jesus is interceding for us in Heaven to maintain our redemption, the Holy Spirit intercedes for us on Earth to make our prayers acceptable according to that redemption.

The Day of Pentecost was the day that God sent His Holy Spirit to breathe life and power into His Church, so that the Church would be all that God intended for it to be. Before God sent His Holy Spirit, the Church was lifeless—no real power. The Church was not witnessing and telling people about Jesus. After the Holy Spirit breathed life into the Church, people began telling everyone about Jesus. It did not even matter if they spoke the same language. They told everyone about Jesus, and the listeners understood. Thousands of people were added to the Church. Miracles started happening.

> *Holy Spirit, you are the one that empowers me to pray life-changing prayers.*

Prayer Points—Open your mouth and pray

✠ Holy Spirit, You are the third person of the blessed Trinity. You are the Spirit of truth, love and holiness proceeding from the Father and the Son. You are my teacher. Teach me to know and to seek God, by whom and for whom I was created. Fill my heart with knowledge and a great love for Him.

✠ Holy Spirit, make me a faithful follower of Jesus, an obedient child of God. Give me the grace to keep the Word. Grant me gifts of the Spirit, in Jesus' name.

"Likewise the Spirit also helps in our weaknesses. For we do not know what we should pray for as we ought, but the Spirit Himself makes intercession for us with groaning which cannot be uttered."—Romans 8:26 NKJV.

✠ Holy Spirit of God, help me in all areas of weakness, be strong in my life where I am weak, help me to be spiritually strong. LORD, make me a spiritual giant in my world, in Jesus' name.

✠ Holy Spirit, when I do not know how to pray, stand in the gap for me. When I cannot pray, Spirit of God, make intercession for me. When I am too weak to pray, Holy Ghost, please pray for me.

✠ Holy Spirit, teach me to pray through problems instead of praying about them, in the name of Jesus.

✠ Holy Spirit of God, turn all my self-imposed issues to blessings, in the name of Jesus. LORD, turn every issue that is troubling me into blessings. Let every challenging situation in my life, become divine blessings.

✝ Holy Spirit, make every instrument used by the enemy to frustrate me become impotent and useless, in the name of Jesus.

✝ Spirit of the Living God, break down and destroy every spirit of spiritual deafness and blindness in my life, in the name of Jesus.

✝ Holy Spirit, open my eyes to see beyond the visible to the invisible. Holy Spirit, open my spiritual eyes to see what I need to see to overcome. Show me how to win every battle, direct me in all areas of life, in the name of Jesus.

"Now the Lord is the Spirit; and where the Spirit of the Lord is, there is liberty"—2 Corinthians 3:17 NKJV.

✝ There is freedom and liberation wherever the Spirit of the LORD is welcomed.

✝ Almighty God, today, grant me the Spirit of liberty, no more captivity. Holy Spirit of God, help me and my family to live in total freedom of my mind, spirit and body. LORD, give me financial freedom, in the name of Jesus.

✝ LORD, liberate my spirit to follow the leading of the Holy Spirit. Holy Ghost, give us liberty from all generational issues. We shall not live under any generational curses, in the name of Jesus.

✝ Holy Spirit, uncover any secrets that are keeping me bound, in the name of Jesus.

"But if the Spirit of Him who raised Jesus from the dead dwells in you, He who raised Christ from the dead will also give life to your mortal bodies through His Spirit who dwells in you."—Romans 8:11 NKJV.

✝ Let the Spirit that raised Jesus from the dead, give life to my mortal body. Let everything the enemy is trying to kill in my body receive life. Give life to my mind. Give life to my spirit. Give life to my soul, in the name of Jesus.

✝ Spirit of the Living God, come dwell in me, come into all areas of my life. Holy Ghost, I need You to take charge of my life. Lead me, guard me, comfort me, and teach me, in the name of Jesus.

✝ Holy Spirit of God, give life to my mortal body. Let every area of sickness receive life, every area of pain, I command healing through the Holy Spirit that dwells in me, in the name of Jesus.

✝ LORD, anoint my eyes and my ears that they may see and hear wondrous things from Heaven, by the power of the Holy Ghost.

✝ Almighty God, anoint me to pray without ceasing. Father, give me the grace to pray anointed prayers. Holy Spirit, You are the one that empowers me to pray life-changing prayers. LORD, I need the anointing to pray prayers that get answers. Help me pray prayers that produce testimonies, in the name of Jesus. In the name of Jesus, I capture every power behind any career limitation, shame, and career failure, in the name of Jesus.

✝ Holy Spirit, rain on me now, in the name of Jesus. Rain favor on my life, rain joy like I have never known. Spirit of the living God, rain Your glory upon my life, in the name of Jesus.

"For as many as are led by the Spirit of God, these are sons of God."—Romans 8:14 NKJV.

✝ Holy Spirit lead and guide me in every area of life, from the words I should speak, to the spouse I should marry, and the investments I should make. I seek Your guidance and permit You to move on my life, however You see fit.

"Now when they had gone through Phrygia and the region of Galatia, they were forbidden by the Holy Spirit to preach the word in Asia. After they had come to Mysia, they tried to go into Bithynia, but the Spirit did not permit them."—Acts 16:6-7.

✟ Holy Spirit of God, in Jesus' name enable me to be sensitive to Your leading and guiding. I completely embrace You closing doors in my path, and search for doors You have opened. I invite and submit to Your leadership in all areas of my life. Thank You.

"However, when He, the Spirit of truth, has come, He will guide you..."—John 16:13 NKJV.

✟ Spirit of the Living God, show me the truth; show me the way. Do not permit me to be deceived by the enemy, let there be no area of blindness in my life.

✟ Give me divine direction for my life, direction for this season. Show me Your vision for me, help me develop a passion for the vision, and bless the vision, in the name of Jesus.

"But the Helper, the Holy Spirit, whom the Father will send in My name, He will teach you all things, and bring to your remembrance all things that I said to you."—John 14:26 NKJV.

The Holy Spirit teaches us all things.

✟ Holy Ghost, teach me all things, make me very knowledgeable and let ignorance be far from me. LORD bring to my remembrance, what I need when I need it, in the name of Jesus.

"However, when He, the Spirit of truth, has come... He will tell you things."—John 16:13.

✟ Holy Spirit, grant me divine revelation, insight and understanding concerning my life, in the name of Jesus.

✟ Holy Spirit, help me pray according to God's will.—*Romans 8:26.*

✟ Holy Spirit, help me to wait patiently.—*Romans 8:23.*

56

Section 2

TAKING DOMINION: CLEANING MY TEMPLE

Chapter 8

HOW TO PRAY THE WILL OF GOD FOR YOUR LIFE

God does not normally communicate with people through burning bushes, but He does communicate through burning passion using a heart that is on fire for Him, a heart passionately in love with Jesus Christ, and a heart that seeks after Him.

The power of Heaven changes things on Earth. One of the main commissions is, "Thy will be done on Earth as it is in Heaven." All of Heaven backs that prayer. We have an obligation to pray that commission and watch as God makes it happen. This is why we are here on Earth—because God has plans for this place and you are a major part of that plan. Our ministry is to release God's presences into the Earth. *"For the kingdom of God is not in word but in power."—1 Corinthians 4:20.* We do not want to confuse our destiny with our assignment, our destiny is going to Heaven, but our assignment is to bring Heaven to Earth. *"Verily I say unto you, whatsoever ye shall bind on earth shall be bound in heaven: and whatsoever ye shall loose on earth shall be loosed in heaven."— Matthew 18:18.* Holy Spirit came and moved the location of God from external to internal—to live in us. *"The Spirit of Him who raised Jesus from the dead dwells in you."—Romans 8:11.*

We have an open Heaven when we are in the will of God, because we carry God's presence. *"And the Word became flesh and dwelt among us."—John 1:14.* In context, that word "dwelt" means Tabernacle, House, or Temple. We have been permanently assigned to live under an open Heaven. We release this reality into the world through decrees, laying on of hands, acts of faith, and prophetic Words. When you live under an open Heaven, you will see impossibilities bend their knees to the name of Jesus. The Bible says, *"The works of God will praise Him"* —*Psalms 145:10.*

Unbelief can prevent an open Heaven. There was great famine in Samaria so bad that the people ate their own children. In *2 Kings 7*, Elisha came and told the servant of the king that "tomorrow" there would be more than enough food, but the servant did not believe. That officer answered the man of God, and said, *"Now look, if the LORD would make windows in heaven, could such a thing be?"* —*2 Kings 7:2.* The man of God said to him, *"In fact, you shall see it with your eyes, but you shall not eat of it."* —*2 Kings 7:2.*

To operate under an open Heaven, you need divine perspective. You have to stay conscious of an open Heaven and stay conscious of heavenly presences, abilities, possibilities, and the limitless power that you carry.

Satan's power is no match for the power of God in you, but a lesser power may overcome a greater power that walks in ignorance. *"My people are destroyed for lack of knowledge..."* —*Hosea 4:6.* *"That no advantage may be gained over us by Satan: for we are not ignorant of his devices."* —*2 Corinthians 2:11.*

Obedience opens up the windows of Heaven.

An inheritance is free. To increase an inheritance, you have to apply efforts to multiply what you got free. In the Kingdom, you can get what you need without going after it, but you must go after what you want and you must desire to get it. *"And you shall seek me, and find me, when you shall search for me with all your heart."* — *Jeremiah 29:13.* The Spirit of God lives in every believer, but the Spirit of God does not rest on every believer.

The Holy Spirit is there to be revealed. We have the capacity to receive Him into our lives and present Him to our world. The more we pray in the Spirit, the more we see the supernatural in our lives.

If you do not know what you have, you cannot give it away. On the way to the temple, Peter told the lame man begging at the gate, *"...Silver and gold I do not have, but what I do have I give you: In the name of Jesus Christ of Nazareth, rise up and walk."* —*Acts 3:6.* Peter was conscious of the power that he carried, he released it, and healing manifested. The woman with the issue of blood made a demand on what Jesus carried, and she was healed. Jesus said, *"I only do what I see my Father do."* And He wants us to do the same. *"As the Father has sent Me, I also send you."—John 20:21*. He said, *"Heal the sick, cleanse the lepers, raise the dead, and cast out demons. Freely you have received, freely give."—Matthew 10:8*.

There are endless possibilities for the believer. *"Most assuredly, I say to you, he who believes in me, the works that I do he will do also; and greater works than these he will do."—John 14:12*. You have something to give—be bold and release the anointing. Everything in the Kingdom works by faith. Peter operated in this conviction and his shadow healed the sick. Your shadow will always release whatever over shadows you. Every experience that the LORD brought you through is to introduce you to your inheritance. Every experience is to introduce you to the realm that is possible, the realm that is unlimited in pursuit.

It is important that we experience what we believe—transformed people impact transformation, and this brings fulfillment and joy. Prayer is like a key that has the power and potential to open up the heavenly realm for God's people. If prayer is a key, why don't we use it more than we do?

> *Satan's power is no match for the power of God in you*

Miracles happen when Heaven opens. Jesus healed the deaf and dumb spirit, by commanding Heaven to open. *"And looking up to heaven, He sighed, and saith unto him, Ephphatha (ef-a-tha) that is be opened."—Mark 7:34*. The Bible left the Hebrew translation, because of the overwhelming power in it. *"And straightway his ears were opened, and the string of his tongue was loosed, and he spake plain."—Mark 7:35*.

"Bring all the tithes into the storehouse, that there may be food in my house, and try me now in this," says the LORD of hosts, *"If I will not open for you the windows of heaven and pour out for you such a blessing that there will not be room enough to receive it."—Malachi 3:10 NKJV*. Obedience releases an open Heaven.

God wants to pour out an overflow of blessings upon us — more than we can hold. We can see the implication of *"floodgates of heaven."* It is an outpour. *"Praise be to the God and Father of our Lord Jesus Christ, who has blessed us in the heavenly realms with every spiritual blessing in Christ."* — *Ephesians 1:3.* An open Heaven releases blessings and miracles.

Prayer Points — Open your mouth and pray

"If anyone wills to do His will, he shall know concerning the doctrine, whether it is from God or whether I speak on my own authority." — *John 7:17.*

✟ Father, help us to do Your will, and know Your doctrine. May we know Your principles, and follow them all the days of our lives.

✟ Almighty God, I refuse to doubt the voice of the Holy Spirit in me. Father God, help me identify and overcome weakness that hinders Your will for my life, in the name of Jesus.

✟ Let there be re-organization, re-arrangement, and re-routing of circumstances, to fulfill God's will for our lives, in Jesus' name.

✟ Holy Spirit, teach me the will of the Father, that I may ask according to His desire for me, help me to want what the Father wants for me, and be what He made me to be.

✟ Father, remove worldly bondage from my spirit and cast out worldly desires. Let lust of the world be far from me. Father, help me not to crave the things that are ungodly, in any area of my life, in the name of Jesus.

✟ Almighty God, give us the grace to please You. Holy Spirit let all the work of resurrection and Pentecost manifest in our lives today, in the name of Jesus.

"May the LORD cause you to flourish, both you and your children. May you be blessed by the LORD, the Maker of heaven and earth." — *Psalms 115:14-15.*

✝ *Lord*, may You cause my children and I to flourish and may You, the maker of Heaven and Earth, bless us. Father, cause us to be fruitful and whole in all areas of life, let failure not know us. May we enjoy good health and successful relationships, may everything that concerns us flourish, in the name of Jesus.

✝ *Lord*, You are my hiding place. Keep me safe from harm and danger and from every fiery dart of the enemy. Help me stand against the wiles of the devil.

"Not with eye service, as men-pleasers, but as bondservants of Christ, doing the will of God from the heart." — Ephesians 6:6.

✝ I reject every spirit of eye service in my decisions and actions. *Lord*, give me the grace not to be men-pleasers, but to act as the bondservants of Christ, doing the will of God from my heart, in Jesus' name.

✝ We receive the grace to be bondservants of Christ, the grace to make Jesus our priority. *Lord*, give us the grace to make Jesus our top focus, in all areas of life. We shall always do our job, and work, as onto the *Lord*. We

> *Your shadow will always release whatever over shadows you.*

shall be diligent and committed in all that we do. We receive the spirit of excellence upon all our work, in Jesus' name.

✝ Holy Spirit of God, reveal the *Lord* to me in a new and deeper way. Today, I shall hear the *Lord* and have the desire to do His will. I overcome everything that will keep me from the perfect will of God, in the name of Jesus.

✝ Almighty God, let Thy will be done in my life, as it is in Heaven, in Jesus' mighty name.

"And do not be conformed to this world, but be transformed by the renewing of your mind, that you may

prove what is that good and acceptable and perfect will of God."—Romans 12:2.

✟ Let the fire of God melt anything in my life conforming to this present evil world, in Jesus' name. Let the blood of Jesus deliver me from all worldly conformity. LORD, transform me by the renewing of my mind. Let my mind be transformed by the Word of God. Holy Spirit, transform me from the inside out, in the name of Jesus. Holy Spirit, help me prove that good, and acceptable, and perfect will of God.

"And the world passeth away, and the lust thereof: but he that doeth the will of God abideth for ever."—1 John 2:17.

✟ Father, don't let us become history while we are yet alive, but preserve us and sustain us. Don't let any of our family members become history, LORD. Deliver us from untimely death, and preserve our lives from evil attacks, in the name of Jesus. By the grace of God, help us do Your will and obtain everlasting life, in the name of Jesus.

✟ Wherever we are expecting good news, Father, favor us there, in the name of Jesus.

"And that servant who knew his master's will, and did not prepare himself or do according to his will, shall be beaten with many stripes."—Luke 12:47.

✟ LORD, by Your great power, we shall prepare ourselves to do Your will all the days of our lives.

✟ We shall not go against the will of God. We reject anything in us that would cause us to be beaten by many stripes, in the name of Jesus.

"For whoever does the will of My Father in heaven is My brother and sister and mother."—Matthew 12:50.

✟ In Jesus' name, I will do the will of the Father in Heaven, and be the brother/sister of Jesus. Lord Jesus, take me as Your brother/sister, make me a member of Your family, in Your mighty name.

"For ye have need of patience, that, after ye have done the will of God, ye might receive the promise."—Hebrews 10:36.

✟ Father God, today I receive the gift of patience. LORD, give me the desire to endure, ability to tolerate, and grace to bear. Remove all forms of impatience from my life.

✟ I shall do the will of God, and receive His promise, in the name of Jesus.

"Thy kingdom come, Thy will be done in earth, as it is in heaven."—Matthew 6:10.

✟ Almighty God, let Thy Kingdom come, on Earth as it is in Heaven. Father, let Thy Kingdom come in my physical being, in and my spiritual life. LORD, let Your Kingdom come upon my finances, in the name of Jesus.

✟ May Heaven come down on Earth through my life, may the will of God be carried out on Earth in my life. Almighty God, make me a significant part of carrying out Your will on Earth, in the name of Jesus.

✟ In Heaven there is no death, therefore let every good thing that has died in our lives be resurrected, in the name of Jesus. Let Your Kingdom come into our home as it is in Heaven. We receive the grace to be Kingdom minded, for God's glory, in the name of Jesus.

✟ Almighty God, let Your Kingdom come into this country as it is in Heaven. Bring to an end all that is going on in our nation and nations all over the world that does not represent You.

"Now we know that God does not hear sinners; but if anyone is a worshiper of God and does His will, He hears him."—John 9:31.

✟ I bring all my sins under the blood of Jesus, and ask for forgiveness. Father God, hear my prayer, and give me testimonies, in the name of Jesus.

✟ By the great power of God, I forsake any sin that has given ground to the enemy in my life, in the name of Jesus.

✟ My passion for worship will increase, in the name of Jesus.

✟ LORD, give us zeal for worship like never before. I pray that we delight in worship like never before, in the mighty name of Jesus.

✟ LORD, because we are worshipers, may You hear us all the days of our lives. LORD, hear us in the daytime and in the nighttime. In this month, hear us in a new way, in the name of Jesus.

"I will cry unto God most high; unto God that performeth all things for me."—Psalms 57:2.

✟ King of Glory, let there be great performance and manifestation of great things in my life this month. LORD, perform healing by Your grace; perform restoration in my situation, in the name of Jesus. What I am unable to make happen, make it happen, LORD, perform them, and all the things that had been hard, make them doable. Father, perform miracles in my situation, in this season, in Jesus' glorious name. Amen!

Chapter 9

DEALING WITH PROCRASTINATION

Webster's Dictionary defines "procrastinate" as follows: "...to put off intentionally and habitually; postpone, adjourn, and drag your feet about doing something that should be done."

Once again, we need to hear the surprise in the Master's question, *"Why stand ye here all the day idle?"—Matthew 20:6*. Procrastination is perilous (dangerous, unsafe, and risky) because it robs us of that which can never be regained. Procrastination is perilous because it increases the weight of our burdens.

Paul exhorts us to *"redeem the time"—Ephesians 5:16*.

An opportunity unused is indeed an opportunity lost. Let us be determined to take advantage of the opportunities presented unto us. When we procrastinate, we get further and further behind. The longer we put things off, the worse they become.

> *"Then Joshua said to the children of Israel: How long will you neglect to go and possess the land which the LORD God of your fathers has given you?"—Joshua 18:3NKJV.*

Procrastination reveals deeper problems. Joshua asked why some of the tribes were putting off the job of possessing the land. Often we delay doing jobs that seem large, difficult, boring or unpleasant.

The devil feeds on this power, to keep us from moving forward in life. Pray and ask the LORD to deliver you from holding back in possessing your possession. It should be remembered that one can commit sin, not only by violating the "thou shalt nots," but also in neglecting the "thou shalts."

*So whoever knows the right thing to do and fails to do it,
for him it is sin."—James 4:17.*

Jesus noted the urgency of His task when He said, *"I must work
the works of him who sent me while it is day; night is coming, when
no one can work."—John 9:4 NKJV.*

Wisdom is in the parable of the wise virgins: *"At that time
the kingdom of heaven will be like ten virgins who took
their lamps and went out to meet the bridegroom. Five of
them were foolish and five were wise. The foolish ones took
their lamps but did not take any oil with them. The wise
ones, however, took oil in jars along with their lamps. The
bridegroom was a long time in coming, and they all became
drowsy and fell asleep. "At midnight the cry rang out:
'Here's the bridegroom! Come out to meet him!' "Then all
the virgins woke up and trimmed their lamps. The foolish
ones said to the wise, 'Give us some of your oil; our lamps
are going out. "'No,' they replied, 'there may not be enough
for both us and you. Instead, go to those who sell oil and
buy some for yourselves.' "But while they were on their
way to buy the oil, the bridegroom arrived. The virgins
who were ready went in with him to the wedding banquet.
And the door was shut. "Later the others also came. 'Lord,
Lord,' they said, 'open the door for us!' "But he replied,
'Truly I tell you, I don't know you. "Therefore keep watch,
because you do not know the day or the hour."—Matthew
25:1-13 NKJV.*

When we see the value in prior preparation and the peace that
it brings, we will be less likely to procrastinate. Some are guilty of
procrastination because they are lazy. Procrastination abolishes many
good intentions. To continue putting things off shows lack of discipline,
poor stewardship of time, and in some cases disobedience to God.

Procrastination is the cause of many failures. Every day has
twenty-four hours filled with opportunities to grow, serve, and
be productive. Yet it is so easy to waste time, letting life slip

from our grip. Refuse to be a lazy person, sleeping away or squandering the hours meant for productive work. We must see time as God's gift, and seize our opportunities to live diligently for Him. Procrastination leads to an unproductive lifestyle. If a person is not willing to work, he or she can find endless excuses to avoid it. Procrastination is a destiny killer; avoid it at all costs. Procrastination hinders purpose and is an obstacle to success. The less you do, the less you want to do, and this can become a useless and unproductive way to live.

To overcome laziness, take a few small steps toward change. Set a concrete, realistic goal. Figure out the steps needed to reach it, and follow those steps. Pray for strength and persistence. To keep your excuses from making you useless, stop making useless excuses. "Just do it."

Ask the LORD to multiply your resources. Do not just believe for one source of income. God is very resourceful. The soul of the sluggard (sluggish—lazy) craves and gets nothing, while the soul of the diligent is richly supplied.

Prayer Points—Open your mouth and pray

✞ Almighty God, empower me to do the right thing always. By Your grace, I shall be quick to do the right thing at the right time, in the name of Jesus.

✞ Father, grant me the spirit of inspiration and motivation, to get up and do the things that will bring me success. I reject failure from ruling my life any longer, in the name of Jesus.

✞ Every evil power closing the door of my success, I command to end, in Jesus' name.

"He who has a slack hand becomes poor, but the hand of the diligent makes rich. He who gathers in summer is a wise son; He who sleeps in harvest is a son who causes shame."—Proverbs 10:4-5 NKJV.

> One can commit sin, not only by violating the "thou shalt nots," but also in neglecting the "thou shalts."

✟ Let all spirit of slack hand go, be far from me, I shall be diligent in all that I do and be bless with riches, I shall not bring shame to my family or myself, in the name of Jesus.

✟ You are going to pray and command an end to poverty that has come into your life because of slack hands, and procrastination.

✟ Pray and ask the LORD to make you diligent in all your work and to make you rich.

✟ LORD, let my expectation become a manifestation, in Jesus' name.

Decide to respond now, to answer now, to act now, to wait or delay no longer and to cease putting things off. We must not say, "Tomorrow is another day." Life is so short, so fragile, and so uncertain for all of us. No one knows what the future holds. Stop saying, "I will do it tomorrow" Yesterday is gone, today is a gift and tomorrow is not guaranteed.

✟ From this day, I will take full advantage of every opportunity that presents itself to me, I refuse to delay going after all that life has to offer. I shall co-labor with the LORD to move forward to greatness, in Jesus' mighty name.

✟ LORD, give me the grace to do what I need to do while I am able to do it. Give me the grace to make a positive difference, in the mighty name of Jesus.

> *To keep your excuses from making you useless, stop making useless excuses.*

Chapter 10

OVERCOMING LIMITATIONS

Limitations are restrictions, drawbacks, inadequacies, imperfections, weaknesses, snags, obstacles, problems, hurdles, and holdups. Our limitations lead to God's opportunities. How does God want us to view our limitations?

"On the day when the LORD spoke to Moses in the land of Egypt, he said to him, 'I am the LORD; tell Pharaoh King of Egypt all that I am speaking to you.' But Moses said in the LORD's presence, 'Since I am a poor speaker, why would Pharaoh listen to me?'" —Exodus 6:28-30 NRSV. Our limitations are opportunities to trust God and rely on His ability and power. The enemy wanted to use the wall of Jericho to limit the children of Israel as shown in *Joshua 5:13—6:27.* The battle of Jericho featured one of the most astounding miracles in the Bible, and told us that God stood with the Israelites. If God is for you, no force can limit you or stop you.

Prayer Points—Open your mouth and pray

✝ LORD, by Your great power, let Your efficiency take over my inefficiency, and may Your adequacies take over my inadequacy, in the name of Jesus. Let Your capacity overshadow my weakness, in the name of Jesus.

Our limitations are not God's limitation.

✝ LORD, You are a limitless God. Let Your limitless power enable me in all areas of limitation. LORD, let Your power work through me in a significant way, in the name of Jesus.

> *Our limitations are opportunities to trust God and rely on His ability and power.*

✞ My life will turn into a testimony that cannot be disputed or debated. My miracle will be undeniable; my blessings shall be unquestionable, in the mighty name of Jesus.

✞ The blessings of the LORD make me rich, and I am daily loaded with benefits that will benefit me.

✞ This month, I decree and declare that all my dreams and visions will quickly become my reality, in the name of Jesus.

"A man's gift maketh room for him, and bringeth him before great men."—Proverbs 18:10.

✞ Let my weakness be minimized and my potential maximized, that I may move boldly forward to my purpose and destiny. No power shall be able to stop me. No more delay and no more limitation, in Jesus' name.

✞ Father, put me in the heart of all those in position to bless me. LORD, cause them to think about me and move to be good to me. LORD, as You put people every step of the way to help Joseph, let it be so in my life, in the name of Jesus. I call forth every person and resource assigned to assist me, to not procrastinate or hold back, in Jesus' name.

✞ Every good thing that has died in my life is resurrected through the blood of Jesus: relationship, career, health, and breakthroughs, in Jesus' name.

Our limitations are opportunities for God to work healing and blessings: *"He brought them forth also with silver and gold: and there was not one feeble person among their tribes."—Psalms 105:37.*

✠ Father God, bring me out of bondage, and bless me with riches, let no sickness know my family or me, in the name of Jesus.

✠ Today, in the name of our Lord Jesus Christ, may I go from dust and ashes into glory and honor. May God empower me for success and blessings. By faith in Jesus Christ, I take back all that the devil has stolen from me, in Jesus' name. This is my month of divine compensation and divine reward.

"For they got not the land in possession by their own sword, neither did their own arm save them: but thy right hand."—Psalms 44:3.

✠ Father, let Your powerful right hand give me back what the enemy has taken from me. LORD, help me fight every battle that has risen against me, in the mighty name of Jesus.

"Both riches and honor come from you, and you reign over all, in your hand is power and might. In your hand it is to make great and to give strength to all."—1 Chronicles 29:12 NKJV.

✠ I decree and declare I shall escape every trap of the enemy and every evil plan against me shall fail, every plot of wickedness shall backfire, in the name of Jesus.

✠ Every power sponsoring limitation in my life, be paralyzed, in the name of Jesus. I shall not be limited in any good area of life. There shall be no professional or personal limitations in my life.

✠ Anything in my life opening the door for the enemy to be able to hinder me must end today, in Jesus' name.

✠ Any power causing inadequacy, end. There will be no more occasions for inadequacy; by the great power of the Holy Spirit who is my helper, I shall be good enough in all that I do.

✠ All my enemies shall surrender to me; they shall surrender to the power of God that is within me, in the name of Jesus. *"He that is in me is greater than he that is in the world."—1*

John 4:4 NKJV. My God is bigger than every power that is coming against me, physically, spiritually, financially, emotionally. Every power that rises up against me in any area of life, I overcome them all, in Jesus' name.

✟ Let the anointing to excel and prosper fall mightily upon every area of my life, in Jesus' name. By the power in the blood of Jesus, I break the curse of repeated failure working in any area of my life, in the name of Jesus. Let every anti-progress altar working against me be destroyed with the fire of God, in Jesus' name. By the great power of God, I command all evil altars speaking into my life to be forever silent, in the name of Jesus.

✟ I withdraw my blessing from the hands of the oppressors, in the name of Jesus. Wherever my blessing is, locate me by the fire of God. I speak to all my blessings, to gather and come into my life, in this season, for the glory of God.

"Therefore I will look unto the LORD; I will wait for the God of my salvation: my God will hear me. Rejoice not against me, O mine enemy: when I fall, I shall arise; when I sit in darkness, the LORD shall be a light unto me."—Micah 7:7-8.

✟ Almighty God, I look unto You, I will wait for the God of my salvation. As You heard Elijah, may You hear me. Father, do not permit the enemy to rejoice over me. When I fall, I shall arise. This is my year to arise from every fall, in the name of Jesus. *LORD,* be a light unto me, in all areas of darkness. Let there be no more darkness, may the light of God keep me from falling. Father, as You helped Elijah when darkness was trying to overcome him, *LORD,* help me.

✟ Anything standing in my life as a blemish, I command you, in the name of Jesus, vanish now. *LORD,* remove all physical and spiritual blemishes; remove all evil spots, flaws, and stains. Father, remove all demonic marks in my life, in the name of Jesus.

✧ O *LORD*, give me power to break through and overcome every obstacle, hindrance, problem, difficulty, complication, and hurdle to my success.

✧ I take back all my possessions from the warehouse of the strongman, in the name of Jesus.

✧ I claim the power to overcome and to excel among all competitors, by the power of God; I shall win in this race of life, in the name of Jesus.

✧ By the anointing of Almighty God, I have dominion over every satanic challenge in my life, marriage, finances, and ministry. I have dominion, and I take authority over all powers of darkness, in the mighty name of Jesus.

"Thou hast granted me life and favor, and thy visitation hath preserved my spirit." —Job 10:12.

✧ This year, *LORD*, grant me life and favor, grant me the type of favor that will open mighty doors for me, grant me a life that is fulfilled, and healthy. Father, let Your visitation preserve me, preserve my family, and preserve all that concerns me, in the name of Jesus.

✧ Let all decisions concerning me, made by any team, board, jury, or council, be favorable to me, in the name of Jesus. Oh *LORD*, bring me into favor with all those who will decide on my promotion. *LORD*, bring honey out of the rock for me this month.

✧ I remove my name from the book of seers of goodness without receiving it, in the name of Jesus. I shall be blessed as others are being blessed.

"Therefore humble yourselves under the mighty hand of God, that He may exalt you in due time." —1 Peter 5:6 NKJV.

✧ Father, deliver us from the spirit of pride, and self, self-pity, self-centeredness, selfishness, and all about self. Deliver us from putting self before God. Holy Spirit, deliver us, in the name of Jesus.

✞ That which hinders me from greatness, begin to give way now. All demonic chains preventing my advancement are broken. Every imprisoned and buried potential, come forth now, in the name of Jesus.

✞ LORD, enlarge my coast beyond my wildest dreams, in the name of Jesus.

✞ I claim back all my goods presently residing in the wrong camp, in the name of Jesus.

✞ Let every power chasing blessings away from me be nullified, in the name of Jesus. If there is any ungodly scent on me in the spiritual realm chasing blessings away from me, be reversed, and start to draw blessing to me like a magnet, in the name of Jesus.

✞ Let the enemy begin to vomit every good thing they have eaten up in my life, in the name of Jesus.

"But my horn shalt thou exalt like the horn of an unicorn: I shall be anointed with fresh oil."—Psalms 92:10.

✞ Almighty God, may this be the season for my horn to be exalted. I receive anointing with fresh oil of God. I am anointed for breakthrough, healing and for deliverance, in the name of Jesus.

✞ Every weapon that the enemy is using to limit my destiny, be destroyed by the Word of God. *"No weapon formed against you shall prosper, and every tongue which rises against you in judgment you shall condemn."—Isaiah 54:17 NKJV.*

✞ Almighty God, re-organize my life according to Your perfect will for me, in the name of Jesus.

✞ My life will receive the enabling power of God and move forward to greatness, in the name of Jesus.

✞ Father God, by Your great power, let my name and the names of all my loved ones, be removed from the book of losers, in the name of Jesus.

✟ *Lord*, I commit all my work to Your hand. I pray an open Heaven upon my work, upon my career, upon my ministry, and *Lord*, we commit all our work onto Your mighty hand.

✟ From Dr. Pat: Open your mouth and command this day to release good things to your life. Command the good things of today to come to you. All the blessings of today, wherever they may be, call them in, from the North, South, East and West!

✟ Financial blessings, come to us! No more financial limitations, in Jesus' name. Today, I receive increased wisdom, favor, and anointing.

✟ Father God, deliver me from wrong decisions, deliver me from consequences of past wrong decisions and from making future bad decisions. I pray that all my decisions will start to bring good results and success, in the name of Jesus.

✟ I conquer evil with good, I conquer fear with faith, and I conquer shame with honor, in the name of Jesus.

✟ Father, keep me from any loss; keep that which You have given to me. Blood of Jesus, protect my life and property. Father, do not allow my blessings to turn to sorrow, in the name of Jesus.

✟ *Lord*, let there be revision, rearrangement, rerouting of situations and circumstances to create a path to my desired miracles and testimonies, in the name of Jesus.

✟ Every power delegated against my day of joy, I nullify you in advance, in the name of Jesus.

✟ Father God, do something great in my life that will make me sing and dance for joy. Before this month ends, let the good news that I have been waiting for and believing for, happen. Father God, surprise me today, with pleasant surprises. *Lord,* You are the God that cannot fail, all my hope is in You!

✟ I speak to all my battles and command them to turn to blessings. All crooked and difficult areas of my life must start yielding testimonies for the Glory of God, in the name of Jesus.

✞ *Lord* God Almighty, cause all my enemies wherever they are to become afraid of me, because of the anointing and favor of God on my life.

✞ *Lord*, from today I decree that my life will be transformed. Prosperity and ease will replace constant struggle and challenge.

"Thou shalt weep no more: he will be very gracious unto thee at the voice of thy cry; when he shall hear it, he will answer thee."—Isaiah 30:19.

✞ Almighty God, end every source of weeping in my life by Your power. Be gracious to me at the voice of my cry, in the name of Jesus.

✞ Almighty God, intervene in the satanic battles confronting me, cause them to fall apart, cause them to fail completely, in Jesus' name.

✞ Father, let Your anointing fall on my eyes to see and recognize divine opportunities, I will not miss my opportunities and blessings, in Jesus' name.

✞ From Dr. Pat: Receive power to leap over every wall that the enemy has built, in Jesus' name. I command every demonic reinforcement against your life to be broken. Every wall of Jericho must go down, you shall move forward to greatness, in the name of Jesus.

✞ Let every attack of the enemy result in my advancement. Today, *Lord*, turn my mourning into dancing and my tears into joy.

✞ *Lord*, display Your power against unrepentant opposition in my life, as You did for Moses and Esther. Father, convert my opposition to promotion; I shall no longer experience hindrance or sabotage, in Jesus' name.

✞ I cast out the spirit of evil inheritance that is been limiting my family. *Lord* have mercy on my family and families all over the world. Help us where we have been weak, and perfect Your awesome ability, in Jesus' name!

✝ Father God, let Your power be released upon my body from the top of my head to the soles of my feet—let there be no more physical limitation. I shall move forward to the things I have to do and places I have to go, for the glory of God.

"Then said the LORD unto me, Thou hast well seen: for I will hasten my word to perform it."—Jeremiah 1:12.

✝ Father God, hasten to perform Your promise in my life, in the name of Jesus.

✝ My limitations are temporary. By the great power of God, let everything that has been difficult for me to accomplish become easy and doable, in the name of Jesus. Just as Peter, who was afraid and denied Jesus, became bold proclaiming Jesus, I receive the anointing for boldness and confidence, in the name of Jesus.

✝ Father, make my life a danger zone for all those who seek to destroy me.

✝ LORD, give me the grace to hear You regularly—one Word from You can take me to great levels of success and breakthrough.

✝ Today I bind and break all witchcraft curses, spells, hexes, covenants and powers that have been limiting my purpose, by the blood of Jesus.

✝ I command all evil and demonic forces to back off and back out of my life. I disable and disallow all their assignments against me, to keep me from moving forward in life, in the name of Jesus.

✝ I will persist until I succeed. There will be no setbacks, no delays, no holdups and no substitutes to my blessings, in Jesus' name.

✝ This month, Heaven will support me in a new way. May the power of God work for me like never before.

"Except the LORD build the house, they labour in vain that build it: except the LORD keep the city, the watchman waketh but in vain."—Psalms 127:1.

✟ I shall no longer labor in vain; I receive the blessings and help of God in all that I do, in the name of Jesus. I decree and declare that the work of my hands is blessed, in Jesus' name.

✟ LORD God Almighty, this month give me a major business breakthrough. Every incapacity robbing me of my blessing will change into capacity and capability, in Jesus' name.

God does not make a way—He is the way.

✟ Father, make a way for me for the rest of the year like never before. Always go before me, making every crooked way straight, in the mighty name of Jesus.

✟ Father, today, speak to my situation, and cause every good door that has been shut in my face to be open, in the name of Jesus.

✟ I command every power limiting my progress and success to be forever silent. I refuse to be held back and held down any longer by any form of obstacle, for I serve a limitless God.

✟ I walk in dominion and authority, no more limitation, no more sabotage, no more hindrances, and no more delay to my breakthrough, in Jesus' name. Amen!

Chapter 11

USE YOUR FAITH TO GET A DIVINE MOVE OF GOD

W hat is faith? Trust in God. No man was ever disappointed who put his trust in God.

According to Webster's Dictionary, faith is "an unquestioning belief that does not require proof or evidence."

If you can see the invisible, you can do and have the impossible. God wanted Abraham to see the impossible, so he can receive the miraculous. God took Abraham out in the daytime and said to him, *"as far as you can see in land, I give to you"—Genesis 13:14-15 NKJV.* He also took him out at night and told him *"if you cannot count the starts, your descendants will be uncountable."—Genesis 15:5—NKJV.* God was saying to Abraham, "if you can see it, you can have what I have promised you" and that is exactly what faith is. God is supernatural, He is limitless, and He is calling us to be limitless in our thinking. Faith is an important word in the Bible. The promises and work of God become real to believers in faith.

"Now faith is being sure we will get what we hope for. It is being sure of what we cannot see."—Hebrews 11:1 NLT. Literally, the Greek says, *"Now faith is the reality of things being hoped for, the proof of things not being seen."* Faith is only as good as the object in which it is placed. If you want to get through to God, faith is the way to do it fast, no matter what it looks like.

"Lord, increase our faith."—Luke 17:5 NKJV. The disciples said this because they knew it was the same faith that would carry them throughout life. *"For we walk by faith, not by sight:"—2 Corinthians*

5:7 NKJV. Everything the believer does in life is done by faith—all decisions and actions are done because of faith in God. *"The righteous will live by his faith" —Habakkuk 2:4 NLT.*

Faith is not based on what we see or feel; faith is a conscious decision to trust in the ability of God and to rely on the Word of God. Faith takes action even in the face of challenges or obstacles. Faith steps out with confidence that God has our back, that our inability can be overcome by God's ability. Faith knows that God is interested in our affairs and is able to work them out in our favor, if we would trust in His love and grace. Faith sees possibilities, it sees what other people cannot see or believe.

By faith, we believe in advance those things that right now make no sense, but one day will make perfect sense because we will view them in reverse. The world says, "Seeing is believing." God says, "Believing is seeing." We believe—therefore there is manifestation. Faith is as strong as what it is placed upon. If you will trust God, your faith in Him will turn that situation around for your good. He is able and has your best interest at heart. With that combination, you can put your confidence in His promise to do what He says He will do.

Prayer Points—Open your mouth and pray

✝ *Lord* today, I receive the faith for my miracle, I will trust and not be afraid, in the name of Jesus.
✝ Every conspiracy against me shall no longer prevail. May God expose every conspiracy that the enemy is planning against my faith, in the name of Jesus.

There are people whose blessings are intercepted, like the man at the pool of Bethesda. Pray that your blessing shall no longer be intercepted.

✝ Lord Jesus, as You located the man at the pool, may my miracle and testimony locate me, may I stand out for good, and may my name be picked for blessing, in the name of Jesus.
✝ My blessing will not be interrupted or intercepted, because of my faith in the Lord Jesus Christ. No power shall intercept

my miracle, at the edge of breakthrough, and my blessing shall not be intercepted. No one will intercept my testimony. My joy will not be hindered by any power.

When you believe God, nothing will be impossible in your life.

✛ *Lord*, I believe, let all things be possible for me, in the name of Jesus.

✛ Today, I receive the faith to please God. *Lord*, I believe that You are God. I believe that with You nothing is impossible; I believe my case is not too hard for You. Give me the grace to seek You diligently—to seek You with everything that I am. Father, teach me how to seek You with my whole heart, and as I seek You let me find You. In Your presence I shall have fullness of joy, in the name of Jesus.

Faith connects you to God.

✛ *Lord*, by Your great power let me receive a touch from Heaven, let the Third Heaven be open to me, all the days of my life, Holy Spirit, bless me with the gift of faith.

> *The world says,*
> *"Seeing is believing."*
> *God says,*
> *"Believing is seeing."*

It is your admission that you are dependent upon God; that your hope is in Him. It pleases God when you trust Him and no one else. The devil goes after your faith because he knows its importance.

✛ Every faith destroyer, operating in my life, may the *Lord* rebuke you, in the name of Jesus.

Faith is visualizing the future in advance. It is seeing the future in the present. Every great achievement began, when someone saw the possibility in advance.

✟ Lᴏʀᴅ, open my eyes to see into the future with faith in You, help me see potentials and possibilities, in the name of Jesus.

What do you see? What you see determines your future. God asked several times, "What do you see?" Do you see yourself as a grasshopper or a giant?

✟ Lᴏʀᴅ, help me to see myself as a giant in the face of every enemy, help me to always see that "You have my back" in all situations, in the name of Jesus.

Faith is the foundation of Christian character and is an essential quality in the heart of a person praying. Faith must precede prayer, making it powerful and effective.

✟ Thank You Father, for being both able and willing to do what You have promised in Your Word, thank You for the manifestation.

Your faith produces confidence in your prayers. Compassionate, confident, faith-based prayers ignite our hope and expectations, giving us encouragement in the situations.

✟ Pray with faith for this season to be better for you. Almighty God, make this season sweet for me. Make all my experiences as sweet as honey. Lᴏʀᴅ, make my relationships sweeter than ever before, in the name of Jesus.

God made sweet the bitter water of Marah, in *Exodus 15*. Let God turn every area of bitterness into sweetness. Father, turn all bitter areas of my life into sweetness, in Jesus' name. In finances, relationships, career, business, health, any area that is bitter, hard, painful, or challenging, Lᴏʀᴅ, turn them around, in the name of Jesus.

Faith is vitally important in the life of the Christian. It is by faith that you are saved, justified, cleansed, and look forward to the return of Jesus. You please God by your simple faith. Admit your dependence upon Him, and continually seek to rely upon Him and His grace.

God is a now God.

Many times when we are not expecting, we can miss His best for now, today.

- ☩ LORD, reveal Your best to me, open my ears and eyes to see and receive all that You have for me now, in Jesus' name.
- ☩ Believe for something good to happen to you now, today — you could get that breakthrough regarding your prayer.

   How to stay in faith when it is taking a long time: believe every day could be the day for that change, breakthrough, and answer to that prayer.

- ☩ Wake up and say, "LORD, send the answer now." Keep expecting, that is what is going to give you hope, hope will create your faith, and faith will release your miracle. Believe it is your turn for testimony.

We delay things from happing now because we are not expecting it now.

The moment we pray and believe God for now answers, the tide of the battle turns. If you are at the right place without the right frame of mind, you could miss out.

- ☩ Father, I know my case cannot be too hard for You, I now ....
- ☩ LORD, settle my situation today. LORD, let the answer come now, for Your glory, I thank You in advance for it.

   "But the LORD is faithful, who will establish you and guard you from the evil one." —2 Thessalonians 3:3 NKJV.

✛ All the plans of the enemy to make me fail, LORD, disappoint and frustrate them. All their plans to bring me down must fail. All their efforts and plans against me shall fail—let my faith in You turn everything around, in Jesus' name.

✛ If you want to please God, believe Him. If you want to impress Him, believe Him. If you want to be close to Him, believe Him. If you want Him to use you and do great things through you, believe Him.

✛ We receive righteousness by faith.—*Romans 4:13.*

✛ We are saved by faith.—*Ephesians 2:8-9.*

✛ We live by faith.—*Romans 1:17.*

✛ We are justified in Christ by faith—*Romans 5:1.*

✛ We have access to God's grace by faith.—*Romans 5:2.*

✛ We receive the promise of the Spirit by faith.—*Galatians 3:14.*

✛ We do God's work by faith.—*1 Timothy 1:4.*

✛ We wait for the return of Christ by faith.—*Galatians 5:5.*

✛ We stand firm in our belief by faith.—*2 Corinthians 1:24.*

Chapter 12

I SHALL OVERCOME

To be an overcomer, we must be born again by grace, keeping your eyes fixed on Jesus, no matter what. Your trust in Christ is so strong and solid; you are hardly moved by anything. Your attitude about things you have no control over is always, "God has this." You do not sweat the small stuff, and the big stuff you handover to Him for counsel, help, healing, direction, provision, enablement, deliverance and total dependency.

You trust the Holy Spirit to help you overcome temptation and every trap of the enemy. You use the authority Jesus has given you to defeat all the work of the devil. Satan may have power, but God has given you authority, which always overrides power. God is all authority, and you get authority through close proximity to His authority. Satan lost his authority when he rebelled against God and was thrown out of Heaven. God has all power, and one Word from God will destroy Satan and all his demons. The authority we have is because of God's backing. For example, if a five-foot police officer stops a six-foot man, even though the six-foot man looks bigger and more powerful, he has to obey the authority that the five-foot man carries, his badge. We carry in our badge: *"From now on let no one trouble me, for I bear in my body the marks of the Lord Jesus."* — *Galatians 6:17,* and if anyone troubles you, there are consequences because the Word says, *"...but he who troubles you shall bear his judgment, whoever he is."* — *Galatians 5:10 NKJV.*

"No temptation has overtaken you except such as is common to man; but God is faithful, who will not allow you to be

tempted beyond what you are able, but with the temptation will also make the way of escape, that you may be able to bear it." — 1 Corinthians 10:13 NKJV.

Temptation will come, but fear not, God has already made a way out for you. If you will look for it, He is faithful, He is dependable, and He is capable. He knows what you are able to handle. Before it gets to be too much for you to handle, He will always step in. He is a loving Father.

"Many are the afflictions of the righteous: but the LORD delivereth him out of them all." — Psalms 34:19 NKJV. You may be going through — not to worry — you are coming out because of the power of God in you. No matter how many the afflictions are, you are coming out, like Meshack, Shadrack and Abednego, in the book of Daniel 3, you will not smell like smoke. Every believer has a supernatural God, who is behind the scene working out all that concerns them.

Warfare always surrounds the birthing of a miracle and attacks always stand at the edge of your breakthrough. The closer you are to your testimony, the more the enemy intensifies the attack. But you are crossing that finish line, and no devil in hell can stop it, you have come too far. You shall posses your possession, it is your turn, and there is nothing the enemy can do about it!

Prayer Points — Open your mouth and pray

✟ Father, thank You that every affliction in my life is ending. I shall be delivered from them all. This is going to make me like Christ, but it shall not destroy me, in the name of Jesus.

✟ Brokenness is God's requirement for maximum use. Almighty God, for all the challenges and problems, let them bring me godly prospective, let them bring me blessings and promotion, in the name of Jesus.

✟ Open your mouth and command this day to release good things to your life. Command the good things of today to come to you. All the blessings of today, wherever it may be, come. Call in your blessings from the North, South, East and West; command the four corners of the Earth to release their goodness to you, in the name of Jesus.

✝ Today, I receive increased wisdom, favor and anointing.

> *You may be going through— not to worry—you are coming out because of the power of God in you.*

✝ Ask God to deliver you from wrong decisions, to deliver you from the consequence of past wrong decisions, and from making future bad decisions. Let all your choices start to produce good results in all areas of your life, in Jesus' name.

✝ Every power working against my elevation, end, in the name of Jesus. *Lord*, let no one be able to stop my progress in life.

✝ Let no power be able to delay my success in life. Almighty God, let no evil spirit succeed in stopping my purpose, in the name of Jesus.

✝ Father, set my family and me free from all negative forces working against us, in the name of Jesus.

✝ This is one of the most important requests. Ask God to raise intercessors to stand in the gap for you always, in Jesus' name.

✝ Almighty God, let my life be extremely dangerous for the kingdom of darkness.

✝ I pray from today, that my family and I will walk in divine safety. We will not fall into the trap of the enemy. May the *Lord* God Almighty send His angels to battle on our behalf, in the name of Jesus.

✝ Let there be a hedge of protection for my family and me. Father, be our hiding place from the enemy, in Jesus' name.

We conquer evil with good. We conquer fear with faith. We conquer shame with honor, in the name of Jesus.

✝ Heavenly Father, do not let me suffer any loss this day, this week, and for this whole year. *Lord*, let there be no loss of life, no loss of property. Father, keep me from any loss— keep that which You have given to me. Blood of Jesus, protect my life and property.

✝ Every negative word and pronouncement against my success is cancelled, in Jesus' name.

✠ I bind every spirit manipulating against me. Anyone in position to bless me will not hesitate, procrastinate, or holdback, in the name of Jesus.

✠ Yoke of non-achievement, sickness, and poverty, break. Let every yoke of family bondage break, in Jesus' name.

✠ We cancel every form of common failure. *"There is an evil I have seen under the sun it is common among men."*— *Ecclesiastes 6:1 NKJV.* I separate myself from every common failure, I separate myself from common infirmity, common evil lifestyle, and not having success in certain areas; I reject it. LORD, as You separated the Red Sea, separate me from all common evil and failures.

"Every plant that my heavenly Father has not planted shall be uprooted."—Matthew 15:13 NKJV.

✠ I reject all evil plant in my life, I command all evil growth in my body, mind, spirit and soul, to be uprooted, in Jesus' name, they shall no longer manifest. Let all unfruitful plans in my life be uprooted. Any character in my life that is not yielding godly fruit, LORD, let them be removed, in Jesus' name.

Chapter 13

STRENGTH FROM GOD

God is the one that gives His people the strength they need for this journey of life. When we depend on God, we are strong and enabled by Him. He gives us the grace to do what would have been impossible under our own power.

> *"I will love you, O LORD, my strength. The LORD is my rock and my fortress and my deliverer; My God, my strength, in whom I will trust; My shield and the horn of my salvation, my stronghold. I will call upon the LORD, who is worthy to be praised; So shall I be saved from my enemies." —Psalms 18:1-3 NKJV.*

For us to enjoy the strength of God, we need to be bold, take actions, and not be afraid. Fear will limit us if we give into it. God can do great things through us if we receive His strength and courage then step out in His ability operating in and through us. We must be bold, knowing who is backing us up: the Most High God. *"I can do all things through Christ who strengthens me." —Philippians 4:13.*

> *"The LORD is my light and my salvation; whom shall I fear? The LORD is the strength of my life; of whom shall I be afraid?" —Psalms 27:1.*

> *"Be strong and of good courage; do not be afraid, nor be dismayed, for the LORD your God is with you wherever you go." —Joshua 1:9 NKJV.*

Whenever God is calling us to do great things in life, He encourages us to be bold and courageous. He knows that we have a real enemy who will always try to cause us fear and anxiety—who likes to intimidate us. The enemy makes a lot of noise—only noise. *"Be sober, be vigilant; because your adversary the devil, as a roaring lion, walketh about, seeking whom he may devour."—1 Peter 5:8 NKJV.*

God has fully equipped us for the day of battle. We are empowered for every battle we are ever going to face. "We have been strengthened for the day of battle."

Prayer Points—Open your mouth and pray

✛ Father God, throughout this season, I pray for divine strength, divine help, divine glory, and divine accomplishment, in Jesus' name.

"The LORD will give strength unto his people; the LORD will bless his people with peace."—Psalms 29:11.

✛ Father, give me the strength that I need throughout this season, strengthen me physically, spiritually, financially and emotionally, in the name of Jesus.
✛ Almighty God, do not let me experience any form of torture. Deliver me from stress and fear.
✛ Father, lay Your hand upon me today and make me whole, in the name of Jesus. *LORD*, make me whole in all areas.
✛ Father God, do not allow the enemy to hinder my confidence in You. Take power away from all my enemies, in the name of Jesus.
✛ Father God, secure my boldness and courage. Any power harassing me in any area of life, let God defend me, and help me overcome such powers, in the name of Jesus.
✛ Divine promises of God for my life, come forth this year. Father, do not let me miss any of my blessings this year in Jesus' name.

✠ From Dr. Pat: I pray for every student. May God help you in a new way to be successful in your academics. You will not have problems paying school fees or any school expense.

> *God can do great things through us if will receive His strength and courage then step out in His ability operating in and through us.*

You will graduate faster than you anticipated.

✠ From Dr. Pat: May the LORD provide a good job for you if you need one; divine job opportunity come your way—permanent, full-time, with good benefits jobs that will last. Any interview you do shall go well. May you find favor, and be hired. I pray your name will standout to the employer, in JESUS' NAME!

"And He changes the times and the seasons; He removes kings and raises up kings; He gives wisdom to the wise and knowledge to those who have understanding. He reveals deep and secret things; He knows what is in the darkness, and light dwells with Him."—Daniel 2:21-22 NKJV.

✠ Almighty God, You are the one who has all seasons in Your hand. Change my season for the better, change every season of lack to a season of prosperity, change every season of defeat to a season of victory. Father, change the season of failure in my life to a season of success, in the name of Jesus.

✠ LORD, remove all evil kings in my life, and let the King of kings arise and take over my life, in the name of Jesus.

✠ Father God, give me wisdom and knowledge, that I may have understanding in all areas of life. Let the deep and secret things of God be revealed to me by the mercy of God, in the name of Jesus.

"Take away the filthy garments from him." And to him He said, "See, I have removed your iniquity from

you, and I will clothe you with robes."—Zechariah 3:4 NKJV.

✠ Let every filthy garment be removed from my life. All dirty garments, physically and spiritually, I reject you. No more indecent garments on me. By the power of God, I take off every immoral garment, let all garment of shame and failure be permanently removed from me, in the name of Jesus.

✠ Father, be gracious to me and remove iniquity from my life. *Lord*, clothe me with rich robes for Your glory.

"That the God of our Lord Jesus Christ, the Father of glory, may give to you the spirit of wisdom and revelation in the knowledge of Him."—Ephesians 1:17 NKJV.

✠ I receive the Spirit of revelation of Christ, knowledge of His power, His will, His purpose, His anointing, His kingdom, and His peace, in the name of Jesus.

✠ I pray for a major business breakthrough this year, in the name of Jesus—a year to start making great profit, a year to become rich and successful for His glory, in the name of Jesus.

"For I know the thoughts that I think toward you, saith the Lord, thoughts of peace, and not of evil, to give you an expected end."—Jeremiah 29:11 NKJV.

✠ *Lord*, give me the desire that You have for me, and give me the provision for that desire. Let every day of my life be godly and evil-free. *Lord*, let every day this year be trouble-free, failure-free, shame-free, and pain-free, in Jesus' name.

✠ Throughout this season, nothing shall hinder, destroy, or bring me down, in the name of Jesus.

✠ *Lord*, help me to master every day in this season, and have a successful year. Father, give me favor every day this year; let Your blessings be for my family and me every day this year. Prosperity anointing, fall upon me, and produce success in all that I do this year.

✝ May God give me grace to do well in everything I do. Let mighty doors be open. I pray that God Himself will deliver my family and I. May He preserve, provide, and protect all my loved ones. I will not lose my children or any member of my family. I decree and declare that this year will be just for recovery and restoration for me in all areas. May God constantly and consistently surprise me with pleasant surprises. I pray God will send His angels to bring me blessings nonstop. May God reveal the deep and secret things to me, by His mercy, in Jesus' mighty name. Amen!

Chapter 14

LORD, DO NOT DELAY

Destiny is a function of time and it is the devil's target. Satan does not attack you because of your past; he troubles you because of your future. The future is his primary target, and he will do everything to hinder your destiny. When Satan sees that he cannot destroy your destiny, he delays it to cause you to lose hope and faith for your blessings. *"Hope deferred maketh the heart sick: but when the desire cometh, it is a tree of life."—Proverbs 13:12.*

Our God is a God of suddenly. He does things unexpectedly, speedily and quickly—when it is your time. God does things at a time we do not expect, in a way we cannot imagine, so He alone gets the glory.

> *"I have declared the former things from the beginning; they went forth from My mouth, and I caused them to hear it. Suddenly I did them, and they came to pass."—Isaiah 48:3 NKJV.*

Prayer Points—Open your mouth and pray

✝ Almighty God, all the good things You declared from the beginning concerning my life, bring them to pass, let them manifest immediately, in the name of Jesus.

✝ You are the God of suddenly. Suddenly bless us, Father, let our breakthrough be fast. Let our prayers be answered suddenly, in the name of Jesus.

✟ If you do not know where you belong, you will adapt to where you are. Do not settle because of delay, you belong in the Promised Land.

"Bow down thine ear to me; deliver me speedily: be thou my strong rock, for an house of defense to save me." —Psalms 31:2.

✟ I thank You LORD for turning Your ears to me, and delivering me from evil. Thank You for responding to me speedily. Let there be no more delay to my deliverance, in the name of Jesus. You spirit of delay, I reject you in my life. I command you to pack your load and get out of my life, in Jesus' name.

✟ LORD, do not let it be too late for us in any area of life. Do not let it be too late for any of our loved ones to be set free and blessed.

✟ You agent of delay, I bind and cast you out of my life. Stay away from my healing. I command you to get out of my life, and I decree there will be no more delay to my family's salvation and breakthrough, in the name of Jesus.

✟ Father, make me a channel of Your divine blessings. May You send Your blessings through my life. Bless me and make me a blessing everywhere I go, in the name of Jesus.

"Hide not thy face from me in the day when I am in trouble; incline thine ear unto me: in the day when I call answer me speedily." —Psalms 102:2.

✟ In all that I pray for, LORD by Your great mercy, answer me speedily. May You not hide Your face from me in the day of trouble. As You were there for Shadrach, Meshach, and Abednego, may You be there for me, in the name of Jesus.

"Then said the LORD unto me, Thou hast well seen: for I will hasten my word to perform it." —Jeremiah 1:12.

✟ *Lord*, thank You for allowing me to see what You are about to perform in my life, may You hasten Your Word to perform it, in the name of Jesus. *Lord*, it is Your Word I am waiting for—bring it to pass with no more delay. Thank You my Father for Your goodness, which surpasses anything I can put in words. You are faithful, kind, compassionate and full of mercy. YOU ARE AN AWESOME GOD!

✟ Father, give me divine solution to my situation. Let there be no more hold up to my testimony, in the name of Jesus.

"I tell you that he will avenge them speedily. Nevertheless when the Son of man cometh, shall he find faith on the earth?"—Luke 18:8 NKJV.

✟ Almighty God, avenge me speedily. You are the just judge. Justify me in all areas of injustices, and grant me vindication. In the name of Jesus, let this be my season for compensation for all the injustice I have endured.

God does things at a time we do not expect, in a way we cannot imagine, so He alone gets the glory

"Then shall thy light break forth as the morning, and thine health shall spring forth speedily: and thy righteousness shall go before thee; the glory of the Lord shall be thy reward."—Isaiah 58:8.

✟ Father, let my light shine for Your glory. I receive divine health by Your great power. It shall spring forth speedily, no more delay to my healing. In the name of Jesus, let the glory of the *Lord* be my reward. I thank You, Father, for it.

"Hear me speedily, O Lord: my spirit faileth: hide not thy face from me, lest I be like unto them that go down into the pit."—Psalms 143:7.

✞ Almighty God, hear me speedily, let not my spirit fail from waiting, do not hide Your face from me. By Your great mercy, I shall not go down.

✞ Let the anointing for spiritual breakthrough fall on us, in the name of Jesus.

✞ Father, by Your great and mighty power, let it be our turn, let our breakthrough break-forth, in the name of Jesus.

Chapter 15

NO MORE HINDRANCES

H indrance: Obstacles, Difficulties, Interferences, Limitations, Preventions, Sabotages and Obstructions.

Hindrance is a major tool that the enemy uses to attack the believer. It can manifest in our lives through two different sources: our fleshly actions and the enemy of our soul.

Do not let sin in your life hinder your relationship with God. When we live a life style of un-confessed sin, it can cause hindrances in our life and hinder our relationship with God. *"But your iniquities have separated you from your God; your sins have hidden his face from you, so that he will not hear"—Isaiah 59:2.* David concurred, knowing from experience that God is far from those who try to hide their sin: *"If I regard iniquity in my heart, the LORD will not hear"—Psalms 66:18.*

The Bible refers to several areas of sin that are hindrances to effective prayer. Our desire to pray and communicate with God is hindered when we are living in the flesh. "Sin will keep you from praying and praying will keep you from sin." *"For if you live according to the flesh you will die; but if by the Spirit you put to death the deeds of the body, you will live."—Romans 8:13.* Being led by the Spirit nurtures a right relationship with God. Then we will be able to pray and spend time with God, without hindrance, and have a smooth line of communication with the Father.

The enemy uses a hindering spirit to attack the believers. This spirit is one that will hinder answers to prayer, causes failure at the edge of breakthrough, and delays answers to prayers. *"Then he said to me, "Do not fear, Daniel, for from the first day that you set your heart to understand, and to humble yourself before your God, your words were heard; and I have come because of your words. But the prince of the kingdom of Persia withstood me twenty-one days; and behold, Michael, one of the chief princes, came to help me." —Daniel 10:12-13.* These evil spirits try to delay, hinder, limit or even stop what God wants to do in our lives. The key to overcoming these evil powers, are persistence, prayer and fasting, doing our best to live for God, and not giving up, on those desires.

"And let us not get tired of doing what is right, for after a while we will reap a harvest of blessing if we don't get discouraged and give up." —Galatians 6:9 TLB.

Prayer Points—Open your mouth and pray

✞ Spirit of the Living God, end every hindering attack in my life, do great and mighty things through me, for me, and in me, now in the mighty name of Jesus.

✞ Almighty God, work for me, let Heaven help me to accomplish great and mighty things, in the name of Jesus.

"Make haste, O God, to deliver me; make haste to help me, O Lord." —Psalms 70:1.

✞ Holy Spirit, do great and mighty things for me. Help me to accomplish the things I normally could not accomplish on my own. Help me to achieve them this season, in Jesus' name.

✞ Father God, let everything that is hindering my glory be consumed. Let nothing interfere with my blessings; let every opponent to my joy fail, in the name of Jesus.

✞ I cancel everything hindering my breakthrough, in the name of Jesus.

✞ Whatever is hindering my promotion, I uproot it in the name of Jesus.

✞ Father, remove everything that is hindering my prosperity, in the name of Jesus.

✟ Anything that is hindering my family's success in any area of life, today, LORD, bring them to a quick end, in Jesus' name.

✟ Almighty God, arise and show that You are my God. Protect me, defend me, and fight for me in all areas of life, in the name of Jesus. LORD, show that You are in control of my life. Control all areas of my life, and perfect those things that concern me.

✟ Almighty God, bless all our efforts with good results, let constant disappointment end in this season, in the name of Jesus.

"For the LORD God is a sun and shield: the LORD will give grace and glory: no good thing will he withhold from them that walk uprightly."—Psalms 84:11.

✟ LORD, give me grace and glory. May You not withhold any good thing from me. Father God, do not let me lack any good thing throughout this year. Let God's grace and glory be upon all that I do, let it manifest in my personal and professional life, in the name of Jesus.

"For I will pour water upon him that is thirsty, and floods upon the dry ground: I will pour my spirit upon thy seed, and my blessing upon thine offspring."—Isaiah 44:3.

✟ There is something about getting water when you are thirsty. King of Glory, bless me, bless my family just when we need it. You are an on-time God.

✟ Father, give me water of Your blessing and quench every thirst in my life. Father, quench every relationship thirst. My financial thirst is forever satisfied, in the name of Jesus. Let every season of dryness come to an end in my life.

> Sin will keep you from praying and praying will keep you from sin.

Let my seed receive the Spirit of the LORD and blessing upon my offspring, in the mighty name of Jesus.

✝ Let it be known that You are God of every area of my life, and greater than everything that can come against me. Father, let there be no more delay to my blessings. Let my breakthrough break forth, in the name of Jesus.

✝ Whatever has been hindering my blessings and progress, blood of Jesus, uproot them in the name of Jesus.

✝ Any power sabotaging good things in my life today, perish, by the power in the blood of Jesus. I shall no longer be held down or held back, in Jesus' name. Thank You, LORD, for total victory.

✝ I break myself loose from all inherited problems; I overcome all generational issues, in the name of Jesus.

"Praise be to the God and Father of our Lord Jesus Christ, who has blessed us in the heavenly realms with every spiritual blessing in Christ."—Ephesians 1:3.

✝ God is our Father. I receive my birthright, to be more than a conqueror—to be blessed to be a blessing. I receive my birthright to be complete in Christ Jesus.

✝ By the great power of God, we shall recover all that we have lost, through hindering spirits; we shall no longer be hindered in any area of life.

✝ We overcome every obstacle. There shall be no more difficulties in reaching our goals.

✝ No power shall interfere with God's plans for me. Let the limitless power of God cause all limitation to my blessings to come to a quick end.

✝ I command all sources of sabotage to be removed from the work of my hand. Almighty God today bring to an end all the failures I have experience due to hindrances, and let the enabling power of the Holy Spirit help me to overcome all hindrances, in Jesus' name.

Chapter 16

THE POWER OF EXPECTATION

E xpectation involves anticipation, eagerness, and expectancy. If you are to turn your dreams into reality, you need to expect the best and expect to win every day that you live. This is a great lesson in faith. If you want to win in life, expect to win every morning when you get up. The Bible teaches us that expectancy has much to do with our faith. Faith is more than hoping, faith is more than wishing, faith is more than desire. Faith is certainty not pretending or you psyching yourself up psychologically. Faith is living in positive expectation. Faith is expecting the best. Faith is an attitude of confidence in God.

When David went out to fight Goliath, he decreed what he was going to do by the power of God. He expected to win. There was not an "if" I will defeat you and cut off your head. David went out expecting victory, expecting to defeat the giant, and that is exactly what happened. He said he was going to cut off the head of Goliath when he did not have a weapon to use. Because of David's expectation, Heaven made a way for Goliath to go down. When David pulled out Goliath's sword and cut off his head, his expectation became his manifestation. *"The expectation of the righteous shall not be cut off." —Proverbs 23:18.*

No matter what the enemy has taken from you, as long as he did not take your expectation, there is hope for change. Thank God for your expectation and that it will become reality. Develop the mind of possibilities. Elijah gave the widow of Zarephath a picture of her possibilities. It produced her expectations of a miracle harvest in her life in *1 Kings 17.* God is the God of expectation: *"Now may the God of hope fill you with all joy and peace in believing, so that you will abound in hope by the power of the Holy Spirit."—Romans 15:13 NKJV.* Hope is different from expectation. When

Faith is living in positive expectation. Faith is expecting the best. Faith is an attitude of confidence in God.

pregnant, you expect, not merely hope, to have a baby in nine months. When you work, you expect, not merely hope, to receive your wage. What we expect in life is what we get out of life. If you expect to win in the race of life, that is exactly what you will get. What are you expecting in this season of your life? Are you ready to win those battles you have been fighting for years? Now is the time. Can you see yourself fulfilled in all areas of life? It can happen if you can see it!

Few people take advantage of God's abundant resources. The Bible says, *"God is able to do superabundantly, far over and above, all that we dare ask or think. Infinitely beyond our highest prayers, desires, thought, hopes, or dreams."—Ephesians 3:20 Amplified Bible.* We tap into the tremendous resources that God has made available to us when there is expectation. We put ourselves in a position to receive change and great things for our lives when there is expectation. God meets us at our point of faithful expectation.

Prayer Points—Open your mouth and pray

"You love righteousness and hate wickedness; Therefore God, your God, has anointed you with the oil of gladness more than your companions."—Psalms 45:7 NKJV.

✞ Thank You LORD, that You have anointed me with the oil of gladness more than my companions; let it abide in all areas of my life. I faithfully expect manifestation, in all that You have for me, in the name of Jesus.

✞ Father, by Your great power, I expect all my buried virtues to be resurrected by the blood of Jesus. Let expected and unexpected favor be mine this season. Let the spirit of favor follow me everywhere I go, in the name of Jesus.

"According to my earnest expectation and my hope, that in nothing I shall be ashamed, but that with all boldness, as always, so now also Christ shall be magnified in my body, whether it be by life, or by death."—Philippians 1:20 NKJV.

✝ LORD, let everything that has caused us shame and pain in the past, start to bring us honor and pleasure, in the name of Jesus.

✝ From this day, I expect Christ to be magnified in my spirit soul and body. May Christ be magnified in all that I do, in the name of Jesus.

"And he gave heed unto them, expecting to receive something of them."—Acts 3:5.

✝ You only receive when you are expecting to receive something. The lame man's expectation turned into manifestation of a miracle.

✝ LORD, turn all our expectation into manifestation. Let our breakthrough manifest, let our healing show up, may all our blessings be unmistakable. We expect and believe for all areas of attack to come to an end, in the name of Jesus.

"Your expectation shall not be cut off."—Proverbs 24:14.

✝ Father God, let my expectation to prosper not be cut off. My expectation for my family's salvation shall not be cut off. Almighty God, my expectation to get a good job shall not be cut off. Today my expectation to be healed will not be cut off, in the name of Jesus.

✝ Ask the LORD to let you experience Him in a new way, pray that He will allow you to experience Him in a personal and supernatural way. This week I receive the grace to experience God in a mighty way, in the name of Jesus.

✝ God's ways of answering our prayers are often far from what we expect. Sometimes God answers our prayers in more effective ways than we expect. Today, let God's better way of doing things take over my ways and bring divine transformation, in the name of Jesus.

- ✞ Father, answer my prayers however You choose. I trust Your judgment. Do it in any way You see fit. Answer my prayer by Your great wisdom, in the name of Jesus.
- ✞ Holy Spirit, arise and control the affairs of our lives. Arise and control all that concerns us, personally and professionally. We depend on You to take total control of our situation, in the name of Jesus.

"Wait thou only upon God, for my expectation is from Him." Psalms 62:5

- ✞ *LORD*, I am waiting on You only, to move in my life. All my expectation is in You, *LORD*.
- ✞ Almighty God, let all Your goodness that You have laid up for my family and me come upon our lives, in the name of Jesus.

Chapter 17

DIVINE HEALING

There is A Balm in Gilead.

"God is pleased when we stand on the Rock and believe that He is unchangeable. If you will dare to believe God, you can defy all the powers of evil. There have been times in my experience when I have dared to believe Him and have had the most remarkable experiences. One day I was traveling in a railway coach, and there were two people in the coach who were very sick: a mother and her daughter. I said to them, "Look, I've something in the bag that will cure every case in the world. It has never been known to fail." They became very much interested, and I went on to tell them more and more about this remedy that had never failed to remove disease and sickness. At last they summoned up the courage to ask for a dose. So I opened my bag, took out my Bible and read them the verse that says, "I am the LORD who heals you"—Exodus 15:26." By Smith Wigglesworth.

"...by whose stripes ye were healed."—*1 Peter 2:24*. The Blood of Jesus paid for your healing!

Just because Jesus paid for our healing, does not mean you will automatically manifest the benefits. You need to reach out and receive what Jesus did for you by faith! Jesus died for the sins of the world, but that does not mean that the world will be saved, only those that receive His gift of grace.

"Bless the LORD, *O my soul; And all that is within me, bless His holy name! Bless the* LORD, *O my soul, And forget not all His benefits: Who forgives all your iniquities, Who heals all your diseases."—Psalms 103:1-3.* We are to bless God everyday for good health, whether healthy or not. As you praise God for healing, it keeps you strong physically and spiritually.

How to receive your healing

Know what is rightfully yours. You need to understand that you, as a child of God, are fully entitled to your healing through the blood that Jesus shed when He was whipped—"By His stripes!" If you do not know that it is God's will to heal you, then you are going to lack faith, and faith is how you receive what Christ did for you. Just like when you were saved, it was by faith you received Christ into your heart and life. The same is true with healing; it is by faith that we receive the promises of God.

Speak the Word of God in faith. Jesus gave you authority to be healed. Therefore, speak to the part of your body that needs a healing, lay your hands on it, and command it to BE HEALED IN JESUS' NAME. As you lay hands on yourself, see the hands of Jesus on top of your hands, and see His glory light shining through your hands, getting rid of all the sickness and disease in your body!

It is written in *Isaiah 53:5* that Jesus was wounded for your transgressions, bruised for your iniquities, the chastisement of your peace was upon Him, and with His stripes you are totally healed.

It is said that Jesus went through 39 lashings on His back JUST for your healing. In those days, 40 lashings was the point where most people died, because the torture was too unbearable for any person to handle. This was not for your sins, this time He shed His blood it was solely for your healing! Your healing means a whole lot to God for Jesus to go through near death torture JUST for your healing! It was for the healing of your body and mind. Your healing was paid for with the Blood of Jesus! Do not let the devil tell you otherwise.

To improve your health greatly, read *Psalms 23, 25, 27, 30, and 91*. When you release these powerful words of God over your life, sickness must leave your body!

Prayer Points—Open your mouth and pray

✝ May the God who forgives all my iniquities, who heals all my diseases, turn to me today, forgive every sin, and release healing and wholeness into every part of my body. I command every ache and pain to vanish now, in Jesus' name.

✝ I command every knee of sickness and infirmity to bow to the name of Jesus.

> *The Blood of Jesus paid for your healing!*

You are the temple of God, in the temple there is no infirmities.—1 Corinthians 3:16.

✝ Sickness can never dominate my temple again.

✝ I command my body to be released from curse of iniquities and infirmities, in Jesus' name.

✝ Let whatever health issues my mother and father struggled with, not be my portion. Father do not allow my children and I to struggle with any generational health problems, in Jesus' name.

✝ Decree and declare every form of disorder in your body—tissues, cells, organs, muscles, and blood—must receive divine order. Everything the enemy is using to torment you, reject it, and God will use it to transform you.

✝ I command spirits of torment, depression, and oppression to pack their load and go. I cover my body in the blood of Jesus.

✝ Let all parts of our bodies be cleansed from the top of our heads to the soles of our feet, with the precious blood of Jesus.

"But to you who fear my name The Sun of Righteousness shall arise with healing in His wings."—Malachi 4:2 NKJV.

✠ Son of righteousness arise with healing in Your wings, and touch me, in the name of Jesus.

"Many are the afflictions of the righteous, but the LORD delivers him out of them all."—Psalms 34:19 NKJV.

✠ Today decree and declare that you are delivered from all forms of affliction, pain, disease and restlessness. This illness will not escape the anointing of God.

"Beloved, I wish above all things that you may prosper and be in health, even as your soul prospers."—3 John 1:2.

✠ Because the enemy brought this sickness, I will recover double. I receive prosperity like never before. It is the will of God for me to prosper and be whole; therefore it shall be so, in Jesus' name.

"The Lord is faithful, who shall establish you and keep you from evil."—2 Thessalonians 3:3.

✠ Sickness is evil and the LORD will keep you from it, because He is faithful. May God give you the grace to do what you have not been able to do, with His divine strength, in the name of Jesus.

✠ Let all illnesses be reversed. I command them to dissipate and disappear by the power of God. No more pain, strain or discomfort in my body, in Jesus' name.

"Every plant, which my heavenly father has not planted, shall be uprooted."—Matthew 15:13.

✝ I command all sickness to be uprooted. Anything in my body that is not of God, must perish, in Jesus' name.

✝ Let every engagement with the spirit of death be nullified, cancelled and come to an end in my life—I shall live and declare the works of God.

✝ I command all spiritual strongmen causing disorder in any form: reproductive organ, brain, chemical, heart, prostate, colon, bladder, arteries, infections, viruses, lupus, sickle cell, cancer, heart disease, diabetes, arthritis, kidney, and every form of sickness. You must vanish now, in Jesus' name.

✝ Command every power that is hindering your perfect health to fall down and die today, so that you may start fulfilling your purpose. You shall see this sickness no more, in Jesus' name.

✝ Command every fountain of emotional and physical pain and discomfort to dry up completely in the mighty name of Jesus.

✝ Every hidden sickness and disorder must come up and come out with all its roots, in Jesus' name.

✝ Be loosed and released from all inherited diseases.

✝ I bind the strongman of sickness. I command it to become weak and die. I receive the permanent, irreversible, irrevocable healing now. Sickness, be gone forever, in Jesus' name.

"So you shall serve the LORD your God, and He will bless your bread and your water. And I will take sickness away from the midst of you."—Exodus 23:25.

✝ It is written that I shall serve the LORD my God, and He shall bless my bread, and my water, and He will take sickness away from me.

"He sent His word and healed them, and delivered them from their destructions."—Psalms 107:20.

✝ In the authority that is in the name of Jesus, I command my healing to spring forth speedily, fast, quickly, and immediately. You sicknesses, hear the Word of the LORD and come out of my body now. Your time has expired, and you must evaporate, in the mighty name of Jesus. I command you to be forever gone, never to return, in Jesus' name. I overcome death by the resurrection power of Jesus Christ.

✞ I decree and declare no flood of the enemy shall be able to break down my defense. "When the enemy comes like a flood, the spirit of the LORD will raise up a standard."—Isaiah 59:19; a standard that they cannot penetrate.

Section 3

TAKING DOMINION: VICTORY OUTSIDE THE TEMPLE

Chapter 18

FINANCIAL FREEDOM

One of the most qualifying promises in the entire Bible is in Psalms chapter 1. The Bible speaks of a righteous man as: *"He shall be like a tree planted by the rivers of water, that brings forth its fruit in its season; whose leaf also shall not wither; and whatever he does shall prosper."—Psalms 1:3 NKJV.* Whatever he does shall prosper! Prosperity does not necessarily mean, you are going to be wealthy. Prosperity means that you live a life of general welfare, where God meets your needs, you are being fulfilled, and you are enjoying the blessings of God.

Learning to ask is vital to acquiring wealth. Receiving is always a product of asking. It is your responsibility and privilege to ask God for financial blessing.

Prayer Points—Open your mouth and pray

✞ *LORD*, bless me with money-producing ideas. I pray for wisdom. Grant me the wisdom that will create the path to my prosperity. Father show me what to do, how to do it, when to do it, and who to do it with. *LORD* give me divine direction, in the name of Jesus.

✞ Almighty God, bless me with the type of insight that will promote me. Bless me with ability that will announce me. Father, give me the knowledge that will open great doors of provision for my family and I, in Jesus' name.

✞ Father, bless me with big financial blessings to be able to bless Your kingdom. Bless me to be able to sponsor missionaries. Bless me to be a great blessing to the poor. Father God, bless me and make me a blessing everywhere I go, in the name of Jesus.

"Beloved, I pray that you may prosper in all things and be in health, just as your soul prospers."—3 John 2 NKJV.

✞ Father, by Your great power, I shall prosper and be in health, just as my soul prospers. I shall be financially secure and have good health all the days of my life, in the name of Jesus.

✞ LORD, I am asking for financial provision. By Your great power, let me receive financial freedom, in the name of Jesus.

✞ *Honor the* LORD *by giving him the first part of all your income, and He will fill your barns with wheat and barley and overflow your wine vats with the finest wines."— Proverbs 3:9 TLB*

✞ Father, I thank You that as I honor You with my income, You will bless me with financial blessing. I determine to seek the Kingdom and it's righteousness and all that my family and I need, will be supplied.

✞ Father God, today I seek divine opportunities and elevation. Help me, LORD, to find them, for Your name's sake. Let me find and receive Your blessings like never before, in the name of Jesus.

✞ Almighty God, I knock at the door of Your resource. Supply my need in a supernatural way. Father, open to me, the doors that have been closed.

✞ LORD, show me favor in business, ministry and career and let me be well compensated financially for the work I do, in the name of Jesus.

✞ Throughout this year and for the rest of my life, there shall be no more financial lack; let there be no more financial dryness, in the mighty name of Jesus.

No force in hell can stop what God is out to do in my finances this year.

"The LORD is my shepherd; I shall not want."
—Psalms 23:1.

✝ Almighty God, thank You for being my shepherd, I shall not want for food, I shall not want for clothing, I shall not want for good health, or good family relationships. Thank You for being the great shepherd that protects me from all economic problems, in the name of Jesus.

✝ Let all financial nakedness come to an end in my life. Let there be no more financial disgrace, in the name of Jesus.

✝ I reject financial disgrace. Creditors will not come harassing me, in the name of Jesus. From this day forward, I am delivered from debt. I shall owe no man anything, but to love them. Thank You, *LORD*, for financial abundance. Thank You, Father, for financial freedom. *LORD*, thank You for financial overflow, in the mighty name of Jesus.

"And my God will liberally supply (fill to the full) your
every need according to His riches in glory in Christ
Jesus."—Philippians 4:19 AMP

✝ Father, may You liberally supply all my needs, fill me with all that I need to overflow, let my blessings be according to Your riches in glory in Christ Jesus. You are my source and resource. Thank You for Your many riches in my life.

✝ As you invest time in prayers, God who answers prayers will intervene in your case, and your testimonies and miracle will manifest, in the powerful name of Jesus.

✝ Father, grant me the power to be fulfilled, power to be successful and prosperous, in the name of Jesus.

✝ Beginning from this hour, may the God of wealth and riches go to work in my life and finances.

✝ Let new chapters of business opportunity open for me. May an amazing career be offered to me, in the name of Jesus.

✝ I command destruction upon every spell and enchantment against my financial destiny. The devourer shall no longer have power over my finances, the thief can no longer steal from me, and the killer shall not kill my financial blessings, in Jesus' name.

✤ This year, my financial blessing and financial breakthrough shall be unstoppable, in Jesus' name.

✤ No force in hell can stop what God is out to do in my finances this year.

"But remember the LORD your God, for it is he who gives you the ability to produce wealth, and so confirms his covenant, which he swore to your forefathers, as it is today."—Deuteronomy 8:18 NIV.

✤ Thank You LORD for giving me the ability to create wealth, LORD help me to create the wealth that will end poverty in my family, with Your great power, I shall create wealth to permanently silent the spirit of lack for my whole family and descendants, in the name of Jesus.

✤ Almighty, I receive the riches that You became poor for me to have, my family and I shall no longer live in poverty, because of Jesus Christ.

✤ Father, I pray any time we need money, let money be available. LORD, do not allow my source of income to run dry.

✤ LORD, bless me with money to use all the days of my life. Let me always have financial freedom all the days of my life, money to pay bills without struggle, money to establish a business, and run ministry, for the glory of God.

✤ I command an end to every witchcraft curse of poverty affecting my prosperity, in the name of Jesus.

✤ Father, open more channels of blessing and income.

✤ Let the LORD end all financial struggles and limitations. Let them expire today.

✤ Let every power of limitation and delay in financial areas come to a quick end in the life of my family and in mine, in the mighty name of Jesus. Let every spirit keeping my family from financial greatness come to an end, in Jesus' name.

✤ Father, end every spirit of stagnancy in my life, in Jesus' name.

✟ By the power of the name of Jesus, I break myself loose of every evil captivity—no more stagnancy.

"And I will give unto thee the keys of the kingdom of heaven: and whatsoever thou shalt bind on earth shall be bound in heaven: and whatsoever thou shalt loose on earth shall be loosed in heaven."—Matthew 16:19.

✟ I bind every spirit of poverty and cast it out of my life, and the life of my family line. I forbid poverty from running and ruling in my family any longer, in the name of Jesus.

✟ I release the spirit of abundance and overflow into all areas of my life. I reject financial lack, in the name of Jesus.

"The blessing of the LORD, it maketh rich, and he addeth no sorrow with it."—Proverbs 10:22.

✟ Father, this year, let Your blessing make me rich spiritually, physically, and emotionally. Father, make me rich mentally and financially in the things of God—make us rich, in Jesus' name.

"Beloved, I wish above all things that thou mayest prosper and be in health, even as thy soul prospereth." —3 John 1:2.

✟ I receive prosperity in my health. I shall prosper in my soul and in all areas of life. In this season, I shall be healthy and wealthy, in the name of Jesus.

✟ Every area of lack, turn into areas of abundance, let all areas of financial struggles turn to areas of ease, in the name of Jesus. The God of Ephesians 3:20 is my God. *"Now to Him who is able to do exceedingly abundantly above all that we ask or think, according to the power that works in us," — Ephesians 3:20 NKJV.*

"A good man leaveth an inheritance to his children's children: and the wealth of the sinner is laid up for the just."—Proverbs 13:22.

✝ The wealth of sinners is no longer laid up, but will come into my life, in the name of Jesus, I shall leave an inheritance for my children and children's children.

✝ LORD, remove hardship and constant worry, and replace it with Your provision and sufficiency, in Jesus' name.

"Thou shalt increase my greatness, and comfort me on every side."—Psalms 71:21 NKJV.

✝ LORD, by Your great power, my greatness shall increase financially. Put me in a position of influence and affluence for Your glory. Bless me and make me a blessing, in the name of Jesus.

✝ I decree and declare that from now on there will be no more occasions for the enemy to mock me financially.

"Let the LORD be magnified, which hath pleasure in the prosperity of his servant."—Psalms 35:27.

✝ Almighty God, I magnify You. Father, take pleasure in my prosperity, I shall prosper physically, spiritually, relationally, and financially, in the name of Jesus. Thank You, LORD, for prospering me and taking pleasure in me prospering.

✝ I shall not be a slave to poverty or lack. I am royalty, a child of God. May God bless me with expected and unexpected prosperity and money. No more financial difficulties, in Jesus' name.

"If ye shall ask any thing in my name, I will do it."—John 14:14.

✝ Almighty God, we ask in the name of Jesus, that You prosper us in all areas of life.

Chapter 19

DIVINE FAVOR

W hen God has a call upon your life, you need favor to carry it out successfully. Favor accompanies God's purpose. *"Praising God and enjoying the favor of all the people. And the LORD added to their number daily those who were being saved." —Acts 2:47 NIV.* We need favor with both God and man to fulfill our purpose. *"And Jesus grew in wisdom and stature, and in favor with God and man." —Luke 2:52 NIV.* More than 5,000 people were willing to stay with Jesus for days without food, to hear His message—that is favor with God and man. Favor causes pain to be temporary; it does not last when you have favor with God. *"For his anger endureth but a moment; in his favour is life: weeping may endure for a night, but joy cometh in the morning." —Psalms 30:5.*

Favor is grace—special grace makes you attractive to others. Favor will cause you to be picked: *"The king loved Esther more than all the other women, and she obtained grace and favor in his sight more than all the virgins; so he set the royal crown upon her head and made her queen instead of Vashti." —Esther 2:17 NKJV.*

We need the favor of God to make a difference in the world. Favor can come when we seek God's face. Favor will turn the tide of the battle. God's favor on David prevented Saul from killing him.

What does it take to have favor? To maintain favor, obey God and freely choose to submit to His authority over you. Be authentic—be real with God. Prayer changes things for your favor. Fasting binds the hand of the enemy and releases the hand of God on your behalf. Stand with courage and faith. Draw close to God with faith in Him. Most importantly, stay humble. A humble heart pleases God. Humility is one of the biggest keys to having favor as it is written, *"He mocks proud mockers but shows favor to the humble and oppressed." — Proverbs 3:34 NIV. "But He gives more grace. Therefore He says: 'God resists the proud, but gives grace to the humble." — James 4:6 NKJV.*

"Thou hast granted me life and favour, and thy visitation hath preserved my spirit." — Job 10:12.

Noah found favor in the sight of God when no one else did, and he and his family were spared from perishing. They were protected from worldwide disaster. Favor will do that.

Favor is what establishes you. Favor is what brings promotion. The Bible says in *Genesis 39:21* that God granted Joseph favor. No matter what the circumstances were, Joseph rose to the top.

Prayer Points — Open your mouth and pray

✠ I surrender my past, present, and future to You, Holy Spirit, in the name of Jesus. Let favor, kindness, help, support, and approval start being mine, in Jesus' name. I shall be chosen for good things. May God grant me preferential treatment everywhere I go.

✠ Do you think your life will be better if people gave you preferential treatment? Of course it would, so believe God for that.

✠ Almighty God, by Your great power, let the anointing of preferential treatment fall upon us; let it bring success and promotion, in the name of Jesus.

✠ From Dr. Pat: Whatever is causing you sorrow, may God turn them all into joy in your life very shortly. In the name of Jesus, may there be a turn of events cornering all areas of your life for the better.

✠ Father, as You chose Esther and used her mightily, LORD, choose me to make a positive difference in the world, in the name of Jesus.

✞ Almighty God, let my life demonstrate Your power; let it display Your ability as You did with Moses. You are the same God.

> *To maintain favor, obey God and freely choose to submit to His authority over you.*

Favor causes God to visit you: *"And the angel came in unto her, and said, Hail, thou that art highly favoured, the Lord is with thee: blessed art thou among women."—Luke 1:28.*

✞ Let the God who located Mary and blessed her among women, locate me and bless me among my people, in the name of Jesus. *LORD*, give me the grace to be fit for Your great purpose, in the name of Jesus.

Favor will get you to a place of romance: *"So she fell on her face, bowed down to the ground, and said to him, 'Why have I found favor in your eyes, that you should take notice of me, since I am a foreigner."— Ruth 2:10 NKJV.*

✞ *LORD*, let Your favor bring the right one into my life, and end loneliness. Father, let Your favor cause the right person to be drawn to me like a magnet, in Jesus' name. I receive the grace to be irresistible to that one whom You have chosen just for me, both in the physical and in the spiritual realm. Thank You, *LORD*, for doing it.

Favor will help you get a mate: *"He who finds a wife finds a good thing, and obtains favor from the Lord."— Proverbs 18:22 NKJV.*

✞ *LORD*, by Your great power, the one for me shall recognize me as the one, in the name Jesus.

✞ Whatever is standing between me and my marital joy, Holy Ghost fire, consume them in the name of Jesus.

✞ *Lord*, by Your power, break every satanic chain holding my mate back from me. Let no good thing be withheld from me. *"No good thing will He withhold from them that walk uprightly."* — *Psalms 84:11*.

✞ Favor will move the hand of God: *"For they did not gain possession of the land by their own sword, nor did their own arm save them; But it was your right hand, your arm, and the light of your countenance, Because you favored them."* — *Psalms 44:3 NKJV*.

✞ Let the mighty hand of God help me possess my possession. What God has for me will not be possessed by anyone else, in the name of Jesus.

✞ Almighty God, may You grant me life and favor. Remember my address and visit my life, in the name of Jesus.

✞ Favor protects you: *"For you, O Lord, will bless the righteous; with favor you will surround him as with a shield."* — *Psalms 5:12*.

✞ I am the righteousness of God in Jesus Christ, therefore, Almighty God; bless me with favor as with a shield. Let Your favor surround me all the days of my life.

✞ When you have the favor of God on your life, you are fully equipped to go through every season successfully. Pray that things will start to work for you during this season, in Jesus' name.

✞ Father, reposition me for uncommon favor in the name of Jesus.

✞ Almighty God, let Your dreams and Your visions for my life happen. *Lord*, let Your will for my life come to pass. As nobody was able to stop Your will in Joseph's life, let no one be able to stop my purpose. Give me divine favor to make them happen. Father God, let me find favor everywhere I turn, in Jesus' name.

✞ Father God, let my life be extremely dangerous for the enemy to attack, because of Your favor upon me.

✟ *Lord*, let my family and I walk in divine favor. Do not let us fall into the trap of the enemy. Send Your angels to battle for us, and show us favor. Father put Your hedge of protection around my whole family, in Jesus' name.

✟ Let there be deliverance in my spirit, soul, and body. Let there be no more failure, let favor replace all areas of failure.

✟ May the great favor of God, meet my financial need. Thank You, Father for supplying all my need. I see it done already, in Jesus' name.

✟ I decree to my breakthrough, "manifest, in the name of Jesus. Let the Almighty God baptize me with uncommon favor, in the name of Jesus. Let Heaven connect me with every divine business connection and manifest prosperity, in the name of Jesus."

✟ My business shall start to flourish, in the name of Jesus. Father, because of Your uncommon favor upon me, make the impossible possible, in the name of Jesus.

✟ Almighty God, let our lives demonstrate Your power, *Lord*, let it display Your glory and goodness, in the name of Jesus.

✟ From Dr. Pat: You have been working and trying hard to make it, but there are some evil powers swallowing the results of your prayers and hard work. Today it will stop. Receive divine transformation by the favor of God, in the name of Jesus.

✟ *Lord*, You are my hiding place. Keep me safe from harm and danger—from every fiery dart of the enemy. Help me stand against the wiles of the devil.

✟ From Dr. Pat: May your life turn into a testimony that cannot be disputed or debated, because of the favor of God.

Chapter 20

DIVINE ENABLEMENT

E nablement is the grace of God giving us divine support by which God enables man to live and fulfill His purposes. Divine enablement is divine intervention for success. The grace of God is Jesus Christ manifesting His power in and through the believer. Indwelling of God is not a right, it is a privilege, an honor, and it is favor. You do not have to be the best person or have the most glamorous house for God to visit you. It takes favor. Say, "LORD enable me to host You in my life, on a permanent basis, in the name of Jesus."

God loves you, chose you, redeemed you, drew you, liberated you, and enabled you—and He is not finished with you yet. God desires that your foremost pursuit be your deepening relationship with Jesus Christ. Purpose and passion, peace and contentment will then characterize your life.

Prayer Points—Open your mouth and pray

✞ LORD, make my voice the voice of deliverance, healing, power and solution for life, in the name of Jesus.

✞ Holy Spirit, build a wall of fire around us that will make it impossible for any evil spirit to come to us again. LORD enable us to be victorious on every side.

"Do you not know that those who run in a race all run, but one receives the prize? Run in such a way that you may obtain it."—1 Corinthians 9:24.

- ✞ *Lord*, enable me to run a winning race. Make my family and me the winners in this race of life, in the name of Jesus.
- ✞ *Lord*, in the name of Jesus, break down every evil foundation of my life and rebuild a new one on Jesus Christ, the Solid Rock. Let it be built on Jesus, the Everlasting Rock, and the One who is unshakable and unmovable.
- ✞ Father God, strengthen my faith and remove anything that will overwhelm me, in the name of Jesus.
- ✞ May the *Lord* anoint my name with special divine favor upon it. Wherever my name shows up, let it receive divine enablement and support.
- ✞ May the *Lord* anoint my name with special divine breakthrough upon it.

Being able to lay down and sleep is God's enabling power: "I lay down and slept; I awoke, for the Lord sustained me."—Psalms 3:5 NKJV.

- ✞ From tonight, my sleep shall be sweet, for every hour that I sleep; I shall be refreshed double, by the power of God.
- ✞ *Lord*, turn every hindrance, obstacle, or blockage put in my way of progress, into a stepping-stone for me to excel, in the name of Jesus.
- ✞ *Lord*, may You overwhelm, overtake, overpower, and engulf me with Your flood of blessings and success, in Jesus' name.
- ✞ May God multiply my money, favor, healing, friends, ministry, business, opportunities, wisdom, knowledge, joy, peace, influence and affluence, in Jesus' name. Almighty God, multiply my resources in the mighty name of Jesus.
- ✞ *Lord* put an end to failure at the edge of breakthrough in my life—no more disappointment. Father grant me favor and success, in the name of Jesus.
- ✞ In financial challenges, *Lord*, give us a miracle. Let there be no more problems paying bills. Let me always have money when I need it, in the name of Jesus.
- ✞ In life challenges, *Lord*, let me always have the provisions I need, and let them always be from You, in the name of Jesus.

✝ *LORD*, intervene in all my situations, if it concerns me, Father feel free to intervene in the name of Jesus. I decree unstoppable advancement, promotion, and success in the mighty name of Jesus.

"Peace I leave with you, my peace I give to you; not as the world gives do I give to you. Let not your heart be troubled, neither let it be afraid."—John 14:27 NKJV.

✝ I pray for the peace of God, peace that is not based on what I have or don't have. I receive the Word of Jesus not to let my heart be troubled or be afraid, in Jesus' name.

✝ *LORD*, deliver us from all unfriendly friends. Expose the manipulation of the manipulators. Father, separate us from all evil associations; keep us from evil friendships and relationships.

> *Enablement is the grace of God giving us divine support by which God enables man to live and fulfill His purposes.*

✝ God will supply all my needs according to His riches and glory in Christ Jesus, not according to the recession, not according to the economy, but according to His riches and His glory.

✝ Today I revoke and nullify every evil judgment passed upon my family and me. I reject all unfavorable judgment. *LORD*, give me divine enablement in all cases.

✝ I cancel every satanic strategy to devour and waste our money. I command it to end in the name of Jesus Christ.

✝ I cancel everything working against divine purpose in my life. I reject every power working against my divine favor. I command you to come up and come out, in Jesus' name.

"I have set before you life and death, blessing and cursing: therefore choose life that both thou and thy seed may live."—Deuteronomy 30:19.

✤ Every success or failure is based on decision, so I receive grace and power to make good decisions and take the right actions, in every area of life.

✤ Almighty God, enable me to choose blessing and life, in every situation, in the name of Jesus. I decree that all my decisions shall be godly, in the name of Jesus.

✤ Almighty God, ignite my prayer life with Your enablement. Let my prayers, start to get the attention of the third Heaven, let it produce testimonies. *LORD*, make me a prayer warrior and a prayer lover, in the name of Jesus.

"Take away all iniquity; receive us graciously, For we will offer the sacrifices of our lips."—Hosea 14:2 NKJV.

✤ By Your great power, take away all our iniquities, and receive us graciously. Our lips will praise You all the days of our lives.

✤ Almighty God of new beginnings, open fresh doors of prosperity for us, in the name of Jesus.

✤ May God Almighty help us defeat all satanic giants in our promised land, so we can possess our possessions.

✤ We refuse to be stuck in our journey to success and progress. We command every desert spirit to end now, today, in Jesus' name.

✤ *LORD*, let favor meet favor, restoration meet restoration, blessings meet blessings, victory meet victory, prosperity meet prosperity, and joy meet joy, in my life. Anointing meet anointing and promotion meet promotion, in the name of Jesus. I receive double blessings in all areas.

✤ *LORD*, please withdraw my family and me from all satanic regulation and domination, in Jesus' name.

✤ Holy Ghost fire, consume the wickedness of the wicked. Let their entire plan against me and my family backfire. *LORD*, I hand over to You, all those who are wrongfully my enemies. Those fighting against me, fight against them. Contend with those who contend with me. This battle is not my battle, it is Yours, *LORD*.

✠ I am enabled in all areas and I seal my victory with the blood of Jesus. *LORD* let Your availability and ability promote me, Father, let Your accessibility and Your capacity elevate me. King of kings may You transform my life by Your readiness and Your power, in the name of Jesus.

✠ From Dr. Pat: Let that which wants to hinder your blessing and greatness be smashed to pieces. May the Holy Spirit expand your capacity and capability, in the name of Jesus.

Chapter 21

RICHLY BLESSED

The blessing of the LORD is the expression of God's goodness and love toward us. His goodness, protection, and favor are examples of those blessings. God's blessings come in many ways. He gives you a miracle where everybody has given up and He gives you peace that does not make sense in the midst of difficulty. The LORD turns what should have destroyed you into what promotes you. He uses troubles we face, to build maturity—to build up our spiritual muscles. The blessing of the LORD is when all our experiences reveal His love, mercy and grace. Blessings reveal who God really is and blessings from God make us grow into becoming more like Him.

"A faithful person will be richly blessed."
—Proverbs 28:20 NIV.

"He has sent me to heal the brokenhearted, to proclaim liberty to the captives and recovery of sight to the blind, to set at liberty those who are oppressed."—Luke 4:18 NKJV.

Our God is very capable of rebuilding broken people and blessing them; that is why Jesus came—it is one of His specialties.

When we obey God, we can trust that He will display His goodness and love to us. Those who are wise will watch for His blessings in all their different forms. God delights in obedience and He blesses obedience.

Have you ever made a decision to obey God as a way of life? I am not talking about obeying occasionally but in every area to the best of your knowledge and ability. Grace enables you to obey God, not disobey.

Prayer Points—Open your mouth and pray

✞ Whether I am at home or at work, or in the store, or in the church, the blessings of the Almighty God will locate me wherever I am. I am blessed coming in and going out, in Jesus' name.

✞ Every power saying that I will not make it this season, be disappointed, in the name of Jesus.

✞ It is written, *"Delight thyself also in the LORD; and he shall give thee the desires of thine heart."—Psalms 37:4.* Father, give me the means to fulfill the desires of my heart. *LORD* make a way, and give me provision for my vision.

✞ Anointing of sudden change, come upon my life, and let it change for the better. Let the change I have been praying for, begin to manifest, in the name of Jesus.

"Yea, the LORD shall give that which is good; and our land shall yield her increase."—Psalms 85:12.

✞ *LORD*, bless me with that which is good, and let the land of my life yield her increase. Father let the good things in life locate me. I shall increase financially, spiritually, and intellectually, in the name of Jesus.

✞ Almighty God, let this season make a positive difference in all areas of my life. Let this season make a positive difference in the life of my family. Father God, let this season make a positive difference in my relationships. I pray that this season will make a positive difference in the lives of my children and my health, in the name of Jesus.

*The LORD turns what should
have destroyed you
into what promotes you.*

"There is an evil which I have seen under the sun, and it is common."—Ecclesiastes 6:1 NKJV.

✝ Pray and reject common financial and marital problems, I cancel all common health and relationship problems, in the name of Jesus.

✝ Pray and forbid all family failures for you and your children. Whatever is making people to fail in my family will no longer affect me, in the name of Jesus.

✝ Father God, let everything that has been difficult for me in the past, become easy and doable. From now on, what has been impossible becomes possible. Let all the things that have been challenging become, easy, in Jesus' name.

✝ Father, close the chapters of sorrow in my life and open new chapters of joy and peace, in the name of Jesus.

✝ LORD, close every chapter of failure and open chapters of success and blessings.

✝ Father, deliver us from those who hate us. Cause all their plans against us to backfire, in the name of Jesus.

✝ LORD, deliver our hands from unprofitable hard labor. LORD, breathe upon our hands and let good things start to happen to the work of our hands.

"I cry out to God Most High, to God, who vindicates me."—Psalms 57:2 NIV.

✝ Almighty God, give me justice for all the injustice that has been done to me, Father, vindicated me, for You are a just God. LORD, by Your great power, justify and compensate me, in the name of Jesus.

God says, "I have a plan for you." The knowledge of God leads to your purpose. God says, *"For I know the thoughts that I think toward you, says the LORD, thoughts of peace and not of evil, to give you a future and a hope. Then you will call upon me and go and pray to me, and I will listen to you. And you will seek me and find me, when you search for me with all your heart.—Jeremiah 29:11-13 NKJV.*

> **"While they were worshiping the Lord and fasting, the Holy Spirit said, 'Set apart for me Barnabas and Saul for the work to which I have called them."—Acts 13:2 NIV.**

✞ Father, show me how to be set apart for You, for whatever You have created me to be and to do. I surrender to Your perfect will for my life.

✞ Almighty God, let the angel bringing my blessings receive divine help to deliver them to me. Let there be no more delay to my miracle and testimony. Angels of blessings and good news, locate me.

✞ Almighty God, this season, reveal Your perfect will for my life.

✞ Pray for the help of the Holy Spirit, so you do not miss what God has for you this season. He is our helper.

✞ Throughout this season, I will not miss my opportunity, let every opportunity I have missed in the past, revisit my life, and this time I will not miss it, in Jesus' name.

Almighty God, wherever we have failed in the past, Father, give us victory and great success in those areas, in the name of Jesus.

✞ Decree and declare that this season will be the season for divine accomplishment in all areas of life.

✞ The evil ones sometimes will put evil marks on people in the spiritual realm to bring all kinds of failure upon their lives, to make people dislike a person for no good reason. LORD, by the blood of Jesus, erase all evil marks in my life.

> **"From henceforth let no man trouble me: for I bear in my body the marks of the Lord Jesus."—Galatians 6:17 NKJV.**

✠ Wherever I have been written off, Father, show up and show out. Show that You are my God. Make possible in my life, what man says is impossible, in the name of Jesus. *LORD*, make everything that has been difficult, easy, in Jesus' name.

✠ Almighty God, just as You used Moses to display Your power, use us to display Your power and Your glory in this season, in Jesus' name.

✠ From today, life will be easy for me. What no one in my family has achieved will be done in my life by the great power of God, for His glory.

✠ Father, from today, open all the doors shut against my family and me, in the mighty name of Jesus.

✠ I destroy every spirit of limitation in my life, in the name of Jesus.

✠ Throughout this season, *LORD*, let me begin to be sought after. Let my gifts and talents start to make way for me, in the name of Jesus.

✠ Whatever the enemy means for evil in my life will all turn to good. May God prosper me in a new way. I pray that Heaven works for my benefit. May God Himself announce me. I pray that my Heavenly Father will advertise me for His glory, in Jesus' name.

✠ From Dr. Pat: I pray God will make this year better than any other year you have ever lived. May this be the beginning of the best seasons of your life. You shall be fulfilled, content, and satisfy, in all areas of life, in the name of Jesus Christ of Nazareth. Amen!

Chapter 22

UNCOMMON BREAKTHROUGHS

A wise man has said it this way: "Wherever people find themselves in life, they usually possess the natural desire to move up. They want greater opportunity, more influence and recognition. They want to earn more money. They want to live in a better home. They want to advance and improve their lifestyle." Failures and roadblocks often discourage us and test our commitment to progress and growth. The Bible encourages us not to give up, but to be persistent in our pursuit for more—not to be greedy or covetous, but just wanting all that God has for us.

> *"Ask and it will be given to you; seek and you will find; knock and the door will be opened to you. For everyone who asks receives; he who seeks finds; and to him who knocks, the door will be opened."—Matthew 7:7-8, NIV.*

If you are believing God for a breakthrough, you must be willing to ask, seek, and knock until the answer is received, found, and the door opened. Pray through, until you see a breakthrough.

We must be so determined about getting an answer that we never give up until God responds. In order to receive a breakthrough in prayer, a person must be willing to persevere and be persistent in prayer. This effort produces breakthroughs. The words ask, seek, and knock are in the present tense. A person is to keep on asking, keep on seeking, and keep on knocking. That means to use prayer as a tool to press in. The Word is telling us, "Do not give up! Refuse to stop praying until you get results."

I woke up one morning feeling like there was an attack going on in the spiritual realm, but I did not know what to pray about, because, I was not sure what the attack was about. I was feeling a great uneasiness in my spirit. So, I asked the Holy Spirit what was going on. I did not hear anything

$$\left[\quad \textit{Never give up until God responds.} \quad \right]$$

clearly. I asked Him what I should pray about. He said, "Pray that the enemy will be at the wrong place at the wrong time." As I thought about it, it made sense—a person at the wrong place at the wrong time will never succeed in their agenda. Ask the Holy Spirit what to pray about. He knows all things. Pray consistently, as you keep talking to God about an issue, He will say yes, no, or not now. Whatever His response is, it is always the best for you at the time.

Prayer Points—Open your mouth and pray

✠ We shall be at the right place at the right time all the days of our lives, in the name of Jesus. As Ruth was at the right place and Boaz saw her, LORD, let our blessings locate us wherever we are, in the name of Jesus.

"If ye shall ask any thing in my name, I will do it."—John 14:14.

✠ Father God, open to me a new chapter of favor and break-through, a new chapter of financial breakthrough. Bless me and make me a blessing in the body of Christ. Let Your blessings overtake me, in the name of Jesus.

✠ LORD, grant us a new chapter of anointing. Let there be a new chapter of business opportunities and breakthrough, in the name of Jesus.

✠ Let the angels of the living God roll away the stone blocking the breakthrough in my life, in Jesus' name.

"And I will make of thee a great nation, and bless thee, and make thy name great; and thou shalt be a blessing."—Genesis 12:2.

✜ Almighty God, as You made Abraham great, *Lord*, bless me and make me great for Your glory. *Lord*, bless me and make me a blessing, make me a blessing in my home, community, in my nation, and in nations all over the world.

✜ Father God, let Your favor add flavor to my life, in the name of Jesus. By Your grace, wherever I show up, use me to make a positive difference, in Jesus' name.

✜ We speak to you, financial mountains. By faith, be made low. We receive wisdom and faith to target an explosive spiritual missile at every obstacle and hindrance, in Jesus' name.

✜ We pray that our overdue breakthrough will manifest by fire. All blessings held up by the enemy, show up in all areas of our lives, in the name of Jesus.

"Be pleased, O Lord, to deliver me; O Lord, make haste to help me."—Psalms 40:13.

✜ Father God, may it please You to deliver me, from all hindrance to my breakthrough, *Lord*, deliver me from all areas of failure. *Lord*, make haste to help me. Let there be no more delay to my breakthrough. Let mighty doors of blessings start to open for me. May the *Lord* be strong in my situation and give me a turn of events, in Jesus' name.

✜ *Lord*, bring an end to financial difficulties. Let all financial challenges be silent. May this season be my season of financial breakthrough, in the name of Jesus.

✜ Wherever we are expecting good news, Father, favor us there. Do not let us be disappointed and do not let us miss our blessings. Let success replace failure in our lives. Let honor replace shame, prosperity replace poverty, and abundance shall replace lack, in Jesus' name.

"I will make you even more prosperous than you were before. Then you will know that I am the LORD."—Ezekiel 36:11 NLT.

☦ Almighty God, make me more prosperous than I have ever been—take me to a new level of prosperity. By Your grace, provide better opportunity for me. Father, by Your great hand of blessing, we would know that You are the LORD, in the name of Jesus.

☦ LORD, let everything that does not glorify You in my life vanish now, and help me get out of debt, in the name of Jesus. King of Kings, help me pay off all my creditors. Let all harassing phone calls end. LORD, I believe You to help me pay off credit card debt, my mortgage, car loan, student loan, and all debt. May they all be paid in full. Help me become a better steward of money, in Jesus' name.

☦ Father God, I shall remember this month for good; it will be a memorable month—the month that I got my breakthrough.

"I have been young, and now am old; yet have I not seen the righteous forsaken, nor his seed begging bread."—Psalms 37:25.

☦ Almighty God, do not forsake me. By Your great power, do not let my children be beggars or borrowers. Make them givers and lenders, and in the name of Jesus, cause them to be blessed in all that they do. Do not let our children be liabilities to others or us. May they all be successful, in all they do. May they make us proud, in Jesus' name.

☦ Financial attack, end now in the name of Jesus. By the great power of God, I come out of every financial tight corner. No more financial nakedness, in the name of Jesus.

☦ Any power, any spirit stopping good things from coming into our lives, expire today, it is time for our breakthrough to break forth, in Jesus' name.

☦ I decree success where any power wants to see me fail, in the name of Jesus.

✟ We decree reversal and cancellation of every strategy of evil force trying to hinder our success, in the name of Jesus.

"Stay on the path that the LORD your God has commanded you to follow. Then you will live long and prosperous lives in the land you are about to enter and occupy."— Deuteronomy 5:33 NLT.

Stay in the path of God's leading to truly succeed.

✟ Father, give us the blueprint for our lives and lead us to our place of blessings. I shall stay on the LORD's path and I shall live long and prosperous in the land of God's promise. I shall possess my possession, in the name of Jesus.

✟ Almighty God, You provided supernaturally for Peter, in his vocation. He got money from the mouth of the fish to pay his taxes. Father provide for us supernaturally. Move supernaturally for us in our vocation—do the unusual, in the name of Jesus.

✟ LORD, provide opportunities for me like never before, and begin to clean away from my life all that does not reflect You.

✟ God of Elijah, arise and empower us for uncommon breakthroughs, in the name of Jesus.

✟ Your assignment and breakthrough will come through the problems God has designed for you to solve for others.

✟ Pray, LORD, show me the problems You have equipped me to solve. Help me solve problems that will open great doors for me. Help solve problems that will promote me and bring financial increase, in the Mighty name of Jesus.

✟ Miracles do not go where they are needed; they go where they are expected.

✟ Almighty God, give us the spirit of expectation, and bring our expectation to pass in Your own timing. Do not permit the devil to delay any of our expectation and breakthrough in this season in the mighty name of Jesus.

✞ The atmosphere you create is determined by the anointing you carry, the anointing you carry determines what you produce. A person can only release what they carry.

✞ Pray, *LORD*, give me the anointing to create an atmosphere of success and wisdom—an enablement to create an atmosphere of freedom.

As a Christian, it is important to tithe to your local church where you are spiritually fed. *Malachi 3:8-11* says, when we give 10 percent to God, He blesses the remaining 90 percent. Tithing produces your seed, and the seed will produce your harvest. If you are not tithing, it could be costing you more than you are withholding. Tithing is not something you do when it is convenient; it is who you are—a tither. For example, you are your gender all the time, not just when it is convenient. Tithing must be regular and consistent for God's tithing promises to be available to you.

Chapter 23

PRAYER FOR MARITAL JOY

Prayer for the blessing of friendship should cover every marriage. Your spouse should be your best friend. A marriage not based on good friendship can be very lonely, and vulnerable to outside interference. In a marriage, men and women have different love languages. Learn your mate's love language. For most women, their love language is attention, support, security and care. For most men, it is sex, respect, honor, and encouragement. Love is important in marriage, especially when you have been married for a while. Many couples stop being romantic. Romance should not be dependent upon whether we feel like it, it should be based on knowing it is your obligation to make your spouse feel loved and valued every day.

When there are arguments, which will happen in most marriages, how do you handle that conflict? You must try to resolve them as soon as possible. Who should apologize? It takes the bigger person, the one who loves more—not just your spouse, but who loves God more. *"Love never fails"—1 Corinthians 13:8.*

Love covers many mistakes and overlooks faults. *"Hatred stirs up conflict, but love covers over all wrongs."—Proverbs 10:12 NKJV.*

Your sex life should remain vibrant and passionate. After having children, some women put all their attention on the children and no longer put effort in having a satisfying sex life with their spouse. Having a fulfilling sexual life can keep your marriage strong and healthy. A man feels good about himself and attracted to his wife when she makes him feel valued, respected and appreciated. A man does not want to be disrespected because he lacks a job or his wife is making more money than he is. One of the things that will motivate a husband to go out and try to provide for his family, is when he gets compliments from his wife about how he is trying, being a hard worker and a good provider for his family. The Bible says, "*...call those things that be not as though they are."—Romans 4:17.* When a man feels neglected at home, it makes him feel like a loser and unsuccessful in all areas of life. This can cause him to be secretly resentful towards his wife, and cause him to withhold, what she wants—his love.

A wife must make her husband feel that he is preferred, admired, and sexy and that she values his opinion. He needs to feel that his opinion is valued in decisions made at their home. It is important for a man to feel that he is in charge and has a say in matters: "*..let the wife see that she respects her husband—" Ephesians 5:33.* Wives, when you submit to your husband as onto the LORD, God is pleased and He blesses

> Romance should not be dependent upon whether we feel like it, it should be based on knowing it is your obligation to make your spouse feel loved and valued every day.

you, your household, and your family. Loving and honoring your husband, is not based on his perfect character, but based on who he is in your life. Of all the billions of women in the world, He chose you to be his wife. After God, He should be the number one person in your life. He needs your unconditional love, as long as you both shall live.

I heard a story about Caroline, who was married to a man. He went out every night, got drunk, came home late, and abused his wife and children. Every night she got angry and told him how bad he was and how shameful he was acting. One day she realized this had gone on for years, she had been praying, and nothing had changed. She decided to change her response to her husband. That night, when he came home drunk as usual, instead of getting angry and fussing, she welcomed him home, helped him change his clothes that were messed up, gave him food, and put him to bed. The next morning he woke up and asked her what happened the night before, because he only vaguely remembered. She told him that she had decided to treat him not based on his action, but instead, to honor him as her husband, and treat him with respect, regardless of what his actions were. She told him that she was honoring him because he was her husband.

The husband, touched by his wife's actions and words, never came home late and drunk again. After years of praying, he became the husband for whom she had prayed—because the angry words were replaced with honor and respect. There is power in your words—you can have what you say!

Men, if you want a wife that you can really enjoy, start to make her feel loved, heard, and cared for. If a woman knows she is loved it frees her to feel safe and secure with you. A woman finds it easier to respect and honor a man who loves her, because she feels safe with him. Women like to know what their husband is feeling and how they can work it out together. If a man wants God's blessings on his life, he must love his wife as Christ loved the church and gave Himself for her. One of the main things that draws a woman closer to her husband, is her husband helping her with whatever she needs help with. God's will for a good marriage is loving, forgiving and submitting to each other.

Unfaithfulness covers issues such as adultery, lusting, people-watching for the wrong reason, pornography, objectification, and obsessing over anything other than the whole person. All of these covet something other than the whole person given to you by God. God wants you to flee from coveting what He gave to someone else, and earnestly covet what He has given you! *"You shall not covet your neighbor's house; you shall not covet your neighbor's wife, not his male servant, not his female servant, nor his ox, nor his donkey, nor anything that is your neighbor's."*—*Exodus 20:17 NKJV* (The 10th commandment), and *"...earnestly desire the best gifts..."* 1 *Corinthians 12:31 NKJV* (covet what God has already given you).

God desires that sex occur exclusively in a marriage. So many marriages have encountered difficulty adhering to this standard. Unfaithfulness is a major problem in some marriages. Unfaithfulness is the ultimate betrayal to a spouse because it damages trust. Restoration of trust takes a long time and hard work. God is very much against adultery and the Bible speaks against it. *"You shall not commit adultery."*—*Exodus 20:14 NKJV* (The 7th commandment) and *"A man who commits adultery lacks judgment; whoever does so destroys himself."*—*Proverbs 6:32 NIV.*

Prayer Points—Open your mouth and pray

✝ Holy Spirit, teach me how to love my spouse. Even when they are unlovable, give me love for my mate. I receive the grace to forgive when there is offense and not focus on short-coming, in the name of Jesus.

✝ Every power working against my marriage, expire now, in the name of Jesus.

✝ LORD, let my spouse have eyes and heart for me only, no other person will come between us physical or emotionally, in the name of Jesus.

✝ I bind every power, and all forces behind tension in my home, I uproot every power feeding problems in my marriage, in the name of Jesus.

✝ Father, deliver my marriage from selfishness and self-centeredness. We receive the grace to be selfless, in Jesus' name.

✝ I cancel all associations between my husband/wife and all strange women/men. Be scattered now, in the name of Jesus.

✝ Every curse working against my marriage, perish, in the name of Jesus.

✝ I pray that whatever problems my parents had in their marriages, will not manifest in my marriage. I reject all generational problems in my marriage. I pray that my marriage will flourish, better than any example I have seen, in the name of Jesus.

"...and the two will become one flesh. So they are no longer two, but one flesh. Therefore what God has joined together let no one separate."—Mark 10:8-9 NKJV.

✝ Almighty God, by Your great power, make my spouse and me one flesh, working together in unity and love. Let no one be able to separate us, in the name of Jesus.

✝ Father empower us with a heart and mind to seek You together, serving You with one mind, one spirit, trusting You for all our needs, in Jesus' name.

"Wives, submit yourselves unto your own husbands, as it is fit in the Lord."—Colossians 3:18 NKJV.

✞ Receive the grace to be a submissive wife, in the name of Jesus.
✞ Let the power preventing me from submitting to the headship of my husband be nullified now, in the name of Jesus.

"Husbands, love your wives, and be not bitter against them."—Colossians 3:19.

✞ Let husbands start to love their wives. Let them receive the grace to fall in love with their wives, and the wisdom to understand and love them, in Jesus' name. *"Therefore take heed to your spirit, and let none deal treacherously against the wife of his youth."—Malachi 2:15 NKJV.*
✞ Lord Jesus, You are the prince of peace. Let there be peace in my home, like never before, in Jesus' name.

"I hate divorce," says the LORD God of Israel."— Malachi 2:16.

✞ *LORD*, because You hate divorce, do not let that happen in my marriage. Help us not to do what You hate. Give us the grace to honor You with our marriage, in Jesus' name.
✞ I command every spirit of lack of friendly communication to end, spirit of constant argument, go, in Jesus' name.
✞ I bind and cast out the spirit of turning every communication into argument. Let my words become sweet in the ear of my spouse, in Jesus' name.
✞ *LORD*, make this marriage a marriage of joy, laughter, and friendship; teach us how to celebrate each other, in Jesus' name.

"Can two walk together, except they are agreed?"— Amos 3:3.

✞ Starting from today, my spouse and I will be in agreement, and we will walk together in all issues, in the name of Jesus.

No power; no spirit will separate us. May the power of God and the blood of Jesus keep us together and keep us close to each other and closer to God.

Chapter 24

PRAYER FOR CHILDREN

The goal of every parent should be to raise their children to know God for themselves: to know Him as Father, Friend, Protector, and Provider. We train them to be able to remember God, in good or bad times.

"Train up a child in the way he should go, and when he is old he will not depart from it." —Proverbs 22:6. Talk to your children daily about God, and display your confidence in Him to your children. *"You shall teach them diligently to your children, and shall talk of them when you sit in your house, when you walk by the way, when you lie down, and when you rise up." —Deuteronomy 6:7 NKJV.* When raising children, it is easy to get so busy with all other things such as career and chores, and forget about nurturing a good relationship between your children and God. This relationship is too important to leave to their teacher, baby sitter or other family members. The most important role in your life is teaching your child to have a relationship with God.

Some important keys in raising godly children are presented here.

Children must be taught accountability to God. They must know that they will give an account to God for every decision they make in life. Your children need quality time with you as they are growing up, so take an interest in every part of their lives. Not every parent has that luxury, because of work, but do the best you can, when you can. It is important for a child to feel loved by their parents, or they may have low self-esteem and go looking for love in all the wrong places. When a child feels loved, they are confident and have good relationships. Your children will have a well-balanced self-esteem when they are built up by your words. What you speak over your children has a great impact in their lives. Parents must frequently speak blessings and life. Pray the words of God over children.

Prayer Points—Open your mouth and pray

✞ Almighty God, give me wisdom to be a godly example to my child. Give me strength and godly wisdom to raise this child according to Your Word. Father, supply what I need, and keep my child walking on the path that leads to eternal life.

✞ LORD help my children overcome temptations of the world and the sin that would so easily entrap them. Don't let them be caught up with the system of the world, but separated onto God, in the name of Jesus.

✞ Salvation—*"Therefore I endure all things for the sake of the elect, that they also may obtain the salvation which is in Christ Jesus with eternal glory." —2 Timothy 2:10 NKJV.*

✞ Almighty God, by Your grace save all my children, with Your great power. Let all my children know You, love You, and live for You, in the name of Jesus.

"Honor all people. Love the brotherhood. Fear God. Honor the king." —1 Peter 2:17.

✞ Father, grant that my children may show proper respect to everyone, as Your Word commands.

✞ LORD, help my children to be humble and submissive to parents and authority. I pray that my children always have a good attitude and appealing personality, in the name of Jesus.

> *The most important role in your life is teaching your child to have a relationship with God.*

"But grow in the grace and knowledge of our Lord and Savior Jesus Christ." —2 Peter 3:18.

✠ I pray that our children would have love for people that will reflect the love of Jesus. May they be drawn to the Savior all the days of their lives. May they also develop social and relational skills needed to succeed in life, in the name of Jesus.

"Children, obey your parents in the Lord, for this is right." —Ephesians 6:1 NKJV.

✠ I pray by the great power of God all our children will be obedient to us; no matter how old they are, they will always respect and honor us as their parents; our children will listen to our wise and godly counsel all the days of their lives.

"Therefore let us not sleep, as others do, but let us watch and be sober." —1 Thessalonians 5:6 NKJV.

✠ LORD help my children to be watchful and sober. They will not do the things that are worldly, but they will be spiritually minded, in the name of Jesus.

✠ I pray that my children will have self-control and self-discipline, and that they be well behaved as godly individuals, in the name of Jesus.

"Blessed are the peacemakers, for they will be called sons of God" —Matthew 5:9 NKJV.

✠ I pray that my child will have the attitude of a peacemaker. When friends or family members bicker and fight, may my children be willing to be a godly influence among them and help set the situation in order.

"I have been young, and now am old; yet have I not seen the righteous forsaken, nor his seed begging bread." —Psalms 37:25.

✞ Father God, do not forsake my family and me. Thank You for the children You have given me. LORD, make them successful, LORD don't let them be beggars or borrowers. They shall be lenders and givers, in the name of Jesus. All my children will be an asset to the world and not a liability. They will be a blessing everywhere they go, in the name of Jesus.

"See that no one renders evil for evil to anyone, but always pursue what is good both for yourselves and for all."—1 Thessalonians 5:15 NKJV.

✞ LORD, may my children always be kind to each other and to everyone else. May they experience personal victories overcoming difficult challenges, coping with unkind people, sibling rivalry, peer pressures, and abuses from adults. May our children stand firm on God's Word to overcome all evil influences, and stay true to Jesus no matter what, in Jesus' name.

✞ Almighty God, my children are gifts from You, LORD I dedicate them to You, let all my children be dedicated to the living God all the days of their lives, in Jesus' name.

"I shall not die, but live, and declare the works of the LORD."—Psalms 118:17 NKJV.

✞ Almighty God, cancel premature death from my children and me. Remove all accidents from their path—sickness shall not know them. Deliver my children from all forms of disaster. May Your divine hand of protection be upon my children. I reject sorrow over any of my children, in the name of Jesus.

✞ Blessings of Children: *"Children are a gift from the LORD; they are a reward from him."—Psalms 127:3 NLT.* Thank You, LORD, for the blessing of my children. Father, let them always be a blessing in my life. Do not let the enemy touch this blessing that You have given my family, in the name of Jesus.

"See that no one renders evil for evil to anyone, but always pursue what is good both for yourselves and for all."—1 Thessalonian 5:15 NKJV.

✞ LORD, bless my children with a heart of love for God and people so they will do no evil. They shall love as Christ has loved us and given Himself for us, an offering and a sacrifice to God for a sweet-smelling aroma."

"Train up a child in the way he should go: and when he is old, he will not depart from it.."—Proverbs 22:6 NKJV.

✞ LORD, let my children stay in the way of the LORD who they know and have been taught, in the name of Jesus. Father, what they did not learn from me, Holy Spirit of God, teach them, in the name of Jesus.
✞ Almighty God, let Your Holy Spirit lead and guide my children. LORD, assist them to grow in wisdom and stature, in grace and knowledge, in kindness, compassion, and love. May they serve You faithfully, with their whole heart devoted to You. May they discover the joy of Your presence through daily relationship with Your Son, Jesus.

"Let integrity and uprightness preserve me, For I wait for you..."—Psalms 25:21.

✞ In the mighty name of Jesus, all my children shall walk in integrity and uprightness all the days of their lives. They will be sincere in all that they do, in Jesus' name.
✞ Help me never to hold on too tightly to my children, nor neglect my responsibilities as a parent.
✞ Almighty God, as I put my children to bed, I pray that You protect them from all evil of the night. Let there be no nightmares. Send Your angels to watch over my children while they sleep. I cancel every manipulation and arrow sent to them. LORD, send down Your angels of protection to protect them

from every evil that roams in the night. I cover them with the blood of Jesus. All these I ask in the mighty name of Jesus.

✠ LORD, let my children not be delayed in any area of life. Both professionally and personally there will be no delay to them achieving and having the good things in life. May they have favor and blessings all the days of their lives, in the name of Jesus.

✠ It is written that children are a heritage unto the LORD. LORD, as my children are growing, lead and instruct them in the way they should go. Protect them from evil and harm. No power seeking to ruin their souls shall prosper, in the name of Jesus. May my children be blessed, healthy and wealthy, in the mighty name of Jesus. I pray my children will be fulfilled and joyful. LORD, Your love and grace are upon my children's lives always. May this prayer for children extend to all children, in the mighty name of Jesus Christ. Amen.

Scriptures to Pray Over Children

Acts 19:20	*I thank You, Father, that Your Word prevails over our children.*
Isaiah 54:13	*that they are taught of the LORD and continue to be*
Proverbs 13:1	*the fruit of godly instruction and correction*
Isaiah 54:13	*Great is their peace and undisturbed composure.*
Proverbs 2:6	*Father, give us counsel and wisdom in bringing up our children.*
1 Peter 1:14	*I say they are obedient, not conforming to the things of the flesh,*
1 Peter 1:15	*but holy, in all conduct*
1 Peter 2:2	*desiring the pure milk of the Word that they may grow thereby.*
James 1:19	*They are swift to hear, slow to speak, and slow to wrath.*
Hebrews 13:5	*Their conduct is without covetousness,*

Hebrews 13:5	*And they are content with what they have.*
Hebrews 13:16	*They do not forget to do what is right and to share.*
2 Peter 3:18	*They grow in the grace and knowledge of our Lord,*
1 Thessalonians 4:1	*And abound more and more in how they should walk and please You.*
1 Peter 5:5	*That they submit to their elders, and to one another,*
1 Peter 5:5	*Being clothed with humility.*
1 Peter 5:7	*That they cast their cares upon You, Father, for You care for them.*
James 1:22	*I thank You that they are doers of the Word, and not hearers only.*
Philippians 1:6	*Effectively sharing their faith*
2 Timothy 1:7	*Not having a spirit of fear, but of power, love, and a sound mind.*
2 Timothy 1:9	*Father, You have saved them and called them with a holy calling.*
2 Timothy 1:9	*Not according to works, but according to Your own purpose.*
2 Timothy 4:18	*Deliver them from every evil work and preserve them.*
John 10:5	*They will not follow the voice of a strangers.*
2 Timothy 2:22	*Flee also youthful lusts; but pursue righteousness,*
James 3:10	*And cursing comes not out of their mouth.*
1 John 5:18	*Because Jesus keeps them safe, the wicked one does not touch them.*
Psalms 91:11	*Give Your angels special charge to accompany, defend, and preserve*
Palms 4:8	*And provide safety for them, day and night.*
1 John 2:5	*Because they keep Your Word, Your love is being perfected in them.*
1 John 2:15	*They do not love the world or the things in the world.*

3 John 1:11	*And they do not imitate what is evil, but what is good*
1 John 1:7	*They walk in the light as You are in the Light.*
James 4:8.	*Cleansing their hands and purifying their hearts.*
2 Timothy 2:22	*They follow after righteousness, faith, love, and peace.*
Hebrews 13:18	*They have a good conscience and desire to live honorably.*
Proverbs 3:4	*Having favor and high esteem with God and man.*

Chapter 25

PRAYERS FOR SINGLES WHO WANT TO BE MARRIED

Praying for a mate is asking God for something He created and called good. *"Therefore shall a man leave his father and his mother, and shall cleave unto his wife: and they shall be one flesh."—Genesis 2:24.* For those who are called to marriage, it is nothing short of asking Him to give you what He wants you to have. No Word of God shall lack power of fulfillment! His authority always backs God's words and we know His words cannot return to Him void. We serve a God who cannot lie. His dreams, vision, and words concerning your life will surely happen. *"And the LORD God said, It is not good that the man should be alone; I will make him an help mate for him."—Genesis 2:18.*

Asking God to introduce you to the one for you, is asking Him to take you from a place of me-focus to a place of us-focus, which is far from being the answer to all your fantasies and desires. Marriage is a training ground for making you more like Christ. Thankfully, in the midst of the training, marriage also provides the opportunity for romance, friendship, companionship, fun, love, and even sex.

Prayer Points—Open your mouth and pray

Jesus said, "Therefore I tell you, whatever you ask for in prayer, believe that you have received it, and it will be yours" Mark 11:24.

✟ *LORD*, I believe. Grant me that one who will be fun and loving to be with. *LORD*, help me not to be selfish, but selfless and ready for a blessed marriage, in the name of Jesus.

> Marriage is a training ground for making you more like Christ.

"No good thing does he withhold from those whose walk is blameless."—Psalms 84:11.

✟ Almighty God, let no good thing that You have made in marriage be withheld from me. Father, make a way for my mate to come into my life, in the name of Jesus.

"Seek from the book of the LORD, and read: Not one of these will be missing; None will lack its mate. For His mouth has commanded, and His Spirit has gathered them."—Isaiah 34:16.

✟ I decree and declare that I shall not lack my own mate. Let my season of singlehood come to a quick end. Let my season of loneliness expire, in the name of Jesus. The promise of "none will lack their mate" is for me, based on the Word of God. No enemy shall be able to stop it from happening in my life.

✟ All the promises of God are yea and amen in him. *2 Corinthians 1:20.*

✟ *LORD*, thank You for all Your promises of yes and amen. I receive the joy to get married. *LORD*, thank You for connecting me to the one for me. Holy Spirit, You are my helper; help me to be with the right person, let there be no more delay.

"He who finds a wife finds a good thing." Proverbs 18:22. The Bible did not say, he who finds a lady, or a beautiful woman, finds a good thing. It says he who finds a wife, that means, a woman who wants to be married, must be a wife, before her husband finds

her—she needs to carry herself like a wife and to talk and act like a one. The Word says, *"...a prudent wife is from the LORD."*— *Proverbs 19:14.*

✝ LORD, make me a prudent wife and let me be one seen as a wife type, in the name of Jesus.

✝ LORD, You created me and I believe You created me for marriage. I do not know the timeline, but I am asking You to fulfill my desire to be married, in the name of Jesus.

✝ I break every wall between me and the one God has for me as a mate, in the name of Jesus.

✝ Holy Spirit of God, You are my helper. Locate my God-chosen spouse and let them be drawn to me like a magnet. I shall be irresistible to the one who is for me, in the name of Jesus.

✝ By the fire of the Holy Ghost, I break free from every witchcraft intimidation and hindrance, in the name of Jesus.

✝ Father God, let no power prevail that would sabotage me getting married. Let there be a scent about me that will be irresistible to my God-chosen mate, in the name of Jesus.

"He will hasten His words (concerning your marriage) *to perform it."—Jeremiah 1:12.*

✝ Father, do not delay in giving me marital joy. Let this be my season of marital celebration, in the name of Jesus.

✝ Let the will and counsel of God prosper in my life, in the name of Jesus.

✝ My life will not follow any inherited evil marital pattern in my family. What my parents did not overcome will not overcome me, in the name of Jesus.

✝ By the power in the blood of Jesus, I shall be happily married. It shall be a marriage full of love, passion, friendship and love for God, in the name of Jesus.

Chapter 26

PRAYER OF DELIVERANCE & SPIRITUAL WARFARE

One of our biggest weapons in deliverance and spiritual warfare is the name of Jesus. I saw an interview of a Nigerian man. He said that he used to be in witchcraft. One year they were having their annual national meeting here in the U.S., and witches from all over the world came. One night they were meeting on the beach, and a man came there to pray. He was walking up and down the beach praying. He could not see them, but they could see him. As he was going up and down praying, he mistakenly stepped on one of the witches, who complained to their leader about this man stepping on his feet. The leader told the witch to go and slap him, so he went and slapped him. The praying man felt the slap and did not know what had happened to him. All he knew was that he felt pain, so he screamed the name of JESUS.

According to the Nigerian man, who was one of the witches at that time, fireballs went out of this man's mouth as he screamed, "JESUS!" They went up to Heaven and immediately came back down, in the form of many warriors with horses, ammunitions and fire. He said as they saw that, they all took off and scattered. The witchcraft meeting that night could no longer continue, just because of that one man calling out the name of JESUS. This former witch said that normally, wherever they hold their meetings, there would be major disasters causing property damage and death. I have always wondered if the man praying on the beach knew what God did through him that night. There is power in the name of JESUS!

Spiritual warfare is resisting, overcoming, and defeating the enemy's lies that he sends our way in the form of deception, temptations and accusations.

Prayer Points—Open your mouth and pray

✠ Let all witchcraft attacks in my life be silent. I nullify every assignment of witchcraft. They shall all fail, in the name of Jesus.

✠ I reject all and any bewitchment in any area of my life. There shall be no bewitchment of my blessing, money, relationship, or in my body, in the name of Jesus.

✠ My Father, carry out a divine surgery that will move my life forward. LORD, take out and cut off anything that is holding me back from Your perfect will. LORD, do spiritual surgery and cleansing. Remove evil attacks from my life, in the name of Jesus.

You will never solve the root of the problem by treating the symptom!

✠ Almighty God, whatever is stopping greatness in our lives, deliver us from it in the name of Jesus.

"But upon mount Zion shall be deliverance, and there shall be holiness; and the house of Jacob shall possess their possessions."—Obadiah 1:17.

✠ Almighty God, deliver me from all things that are keeping me bound. Deliver me from sickness, failure, shame, and reproach. LORD, deliver me from sin, and the consequences of sin, in the name of Jesus.

✠ Every power imposing sluggishness on my breakthroughs, you must perish, in the name of Jesus.

✠ We shall not die unfruitful, unfulfilled, or lonely, in the name of Jesus. Any spirit, and any power that has been keeping us unfruitful, unfulfilled, or lonely, expire, in the name of Jesus.

✠ I receive the anointing to disgrace every utterance of darkness assigned to derail me, in the name of Jesus. I refuse to be ruined by any evil words. No demonic words shall disrupt me this year, in the name of Jesus. Every word spoken against me from the kingdom of darkness shall pass over and not manifest in my life, in the name of Jesus.

☦ God of Elijah, arise! Give me grace and end disgrace in my life, in the name of Jesus. Father, arise and cause failures to fail. Let all forms of sickness in my body fail, in the name of Jesus. Whatever the enemy meant for harm, they shall all fail and turn into blessings.

☦ My Father, arise with Your sword of fire and uproot any evil plant growing in my life, in the name of Jesus. It is written, *"Every plant, which my heavenly Father hath not planted, shall be rooted up"—Matthew 15:13 NKJV.*

☦ Wherever satanic agents are gathered against us, your time is up. Be scattered unto desolation, in the name of Jesus.

"How God anointed Jesus of Nazareth with the Holy Ghost and with power: who went about doing good, and healing all that were oppressed of the devil; for God was with him."—Acts 10:38 NKJV.

☦ Almighty God, as You anointed Jesus of Nazareth with the Holy Ghost and with power, anoint us to also go about doing good and healing all that are oppressed of the devil, and be with us.

If we have a spiritual problem, find the root of that problem and treat it.

Once the root is cleaned up, the problem will not be returning and causing more problems! You will never solve the root of the problem by treating the symptom! Step one is to find the root of problem. Ask the Holy Spirit to show you, and then get serious about getting rid of the problem with the power of God. Fast, pray, and stay close to God, through the Word and prayer. Then verbally renounce, denounce, and break any unclean ties, in Jesus' name. You must verbally renounce, denounce, and break all evil covenants in Jesus' name.

✟ Every spiritual worm eating up our blessings and elevation, perish now, in Jesus' name.

✟ All our hidden treasures buried in secret, come forth now, in the name of Jesus.

"Be pleased, O Lord, to deliver me; O Lord, make haste to help me." —Psalms 40:13.

✟ My deliverance shall no longer be delayed, held back, hindered or sabotaged, in the name of Jesus.

✟ Opportunity killers, I destroy your powers, in the name of Jesus.

✟ Yokes assigned to frustrate our efforts, fall and fail, in the name of Jesus.

✟ Evil power working against our purpose, you must wither, in the name of Jesus.

✟ Any invisible chain holding us back, break, in the name of Jesus.

✟ Barriers and strongholds erected to stop us, scatter, in the name of Jesus.

✟ Anointing for victory and joy, fall upon our lives, in the name of Jesus.

✟ Oil of favor from Heaven, baptize my life, in the name of Jesus.

✟ Let every assignment contrary to blessing be revised, in Jesus' name. Let failure, sickness, shame, depression, loneliness, poverty, rejection and joblessness be revised, in Jesus' name.

✟ Lord, turn us into untouchable hot coals of fire. Surround us with Holy Ghost fire—fire that will keep all evil far from us, in the name of Jesus.

✟ Let our lives be extremely dangerous for the kingdom of darkness.

✟ Every tree of problem in my life, I command you to dry up from your root.

"Though thou exalt thyself as the eagle, and though thou set thy nest among the stars, thence will I bring thee down, saith the LORD."—Obadiah 1:4 NKJV.

✞ LORD, bring down all powers of darkness coming against Your people. Bring them down to nothing, paralyze all their power, veto their plans, and make their agenda useless.

✞ Father God, frustrate and disappoint all satanic agents. Command all demonic activities against my calling, to receive disgrace.

✞ Worms are spiritual eaters of blessings. They are tools of Satan. I drink spiritual divine worm destroyer—the Word of God. I command all evil shrines, altars in the land, in the air, and in the sea, to receive the fire of God and be burned to ashes, in Jesus' name.

✞ I bust my way through every evil roadblock to my miracles, breakthrough, and testimonies, in the name of Jesus.

For those tormented by the spirit of "almost there but never getting there," we are going to break that.

✞ I plead for mercy in all areas of sin and rebellion. I receive the blood of Jesus to cover all my sins, in the name of Jesus.

✞ I draw upon the person of the Holy Spirit, that He may guide me to pray spiritual warfare prayers in wisdom and power, in the name of Jesus Christ.

✞ I break and loose myself from the awful bondage of the power of darkness put upon me to stop my breakthrough from breaking forth. I bind and cast out of my life, failure at the edge of breakthrough.

✞ I reject every force assigned to limit me, delay my blessings, hinder my progress, or end my life, in the name of Jesus.

"They cried out to God in the battle. He heeded their prayer, because they put their trust in Him."
—1 Chronicles 5:20 NKJV.

✝ *Lord*, I am crying out to You in this battle, hear my prayers and fight for me, help me overcome all attackers, in the name of Jesus. I forbid the destroyer's curses from working any more evil in my life.

✝ "Warfare always surrounds the birth of a miracle. Crisis always occurs at the curve of change" Mike Murdock

Attacks allow us to experience the dread of failure at the very point where success is ready to burst forth, to drag our faith and the name of God through the mud. If you have been experiencing failure at the edge of your success, then you need divine intervention through prayer.

✝ Almighty God, arise, let all the enemies standing on my path of breakthrough be scattered, Arise, O *Lord*, let my enemies be scattered, in the name of Jesus.

✝ In the name of Jesus, I smash and pull down the entire stronghold Satan has erected to hinder me, at the edge of my miracle. I pull down Satan's plan to hinder, delay, sabotage, or divert my miracle—he shall not prevail any longer, in Jesus' name.

"Resist the devil, and he will flee from you."
—James 4:7.

✝ I resist you, devil, therefore I command you to flee from me, in Jesus' name.

✝ The pregnancy of good things within me will not be aborted by any contrary power, in the name of Jesus.

✝ Father, turn all my blessings and breakthrough into untouchable coals of fire.

✝ Every evil spirit that has been troubling me, I command you and your plans to catch fire and burn to ashes, in the name of Jesus.

✝ I speak to all unprofitable heaviness in my life that is holding me back from greatness, be cast out, by the power of the blood of Jesus.

✠ I decree and declare that every spirit that is manipulating my divine helper shall be frustrated and exposed, in the name of Jesus. I bind every Jezebel spirit fighting to keep me down and unfulfilled, and I command them to fail in all their plans, in the name of Jesus.

"In this manner, therefore, pray... deliver us from the evil one."—Matthew 6:13 NKJV.

✠ Father, deliver us from the evil ones and from every work of the devil. Deliver us from all his demons, assistants, agents, and tricks, in the name of Jesus.

"For this purpose the Son of God was manifested, that He might destroy the works of the devil."—1 John 3:8.

✠ LORD, destroy every work of the devil in my life. Destroy the work of the devil that has affected my life negatively. Do not permit the devil to hinder my destiny any longer.
✠ Any damage done to my destiny, receive divine repair. The enemy will not convert my destiny to failure, in the name of Jesus.
✠ LORD, restore my family and I to Your original plan for us. We shall no longer operate below our divine destiny.
✠ I forbid satanic prayer from coming to pass in my life.

"And the God of peace shall bruise Satan under your feet shortly."—Romans 16:20 NKJV.

✠ God of peace, bruise Satan and all his work and workers under my feet, in the name of Jesus. Let the blood of Jesus destroy every work of Satan working against my destiny: strongman, familiar spirits, marine spirits, principalities and powers.
✠ Let the fire of God destroy every altar that is speaking and releasing evil into my life. I command every altar releasing curses into my life to catch fire and burn to ashes.

✝ Father, expose the power behind my problems and forever destroy them, in the name of Jesus. Expose every witchcraft power and paralyze them.

✝ Blood of Jesus separate me from every power that is feeding problems and failures in any area of my life, in the mighty name of Jesus.

✝ Holy Ghost fire, purge my life completely. Remove and cast out all evil deposits, in the name of Jesus.

✝ Father, anoint me to come into divine purpose. Satan, I resist and rebuke your effort to change my destiny, in Jesus' name. I refuse to live below God's divine standard, in the name of Jesus.

✝ I paralyze all satanic antagonism against my destiny from the womb, may all their agenda no longer prevail in my life, in Jesus' name.

The pregnancy of good things within me will not be aborted by any contrary power

✝ I take authority over every satanic attack on my advancement, progress, elevation, promotion, and success.

✝ LORD, expose all unfriendly friends who are working against my life. LORD, stop the work of every household enemy, in the name of Jesus.

✝ Let all satanic computers and operators working against me, receive spiritual virus of permanent destruction, in Jesus' name.

"In my name shall they cast out devils."
—Mark 16:17 NKJV.

✝ Almighty God, at the mention of the name of Jesus, let every work of the devil in my life come to a quick end, in the name of Jesus.

✝ I disconnect myself from all satanic monitoring devices being used to monitor my life, in Jesus.

"Get thee behind me, Satan: thou art an offence unto me."—Matthew 16:23.

✛ I command every representative of Satan to get behind Jesus. Whatever Satan is using to access my life, get behind Jesus and never again manifest in any area of my life, in the name of Jesus.

✛ All satanic networks obstructing my blessings, fire of God, burn them to ashes, in the name of Jesus.

"Behold, they shall surely gather together, but not by me: whosoever shall gather together against thee shall fall for thy sake."—Isaiah 54:15.

✛ You stubborn rebellious spirit working against my life, I reject and forbid you gathering against me, by the blood of Jesus.

✛ Break curses, soul ties, and demonic ties.

✛ LORD deliver me from all evil soul ties, I disconnect my soul from all wrong soul ties. I renounce and denounce every satanic soul tie. I decree and declare that my soul is healed and whole, in Jesus' name.

✛ Today, I destroy all evil covenants that have prospered in my life so far, in Jesus' name.

✛ After today, my life becomes impossible for the enemy to touch, in the name of Jesus.

✛ All damage done to me in my dreams; let the blood of Jesus start to fix and repair them now, in Jesus' name.

✛ My soul rejects every evil summons, in the name of Jesus. Evil summons for my soul and the souls of my children shall all fail. Holy Spirit of God, deliver our souls from demonic captivity.

✛ The fires of God flush out every poison introduced into my life through dreams.

✛ Any dreams attached to problems in my life, I nullify you, in the name of Jesus.

✛ By the power of the Holy Ghost, I break loose and break free from problems of evil forces. I receive divine solution.

✛ The grace of God is sufficient for me. I shall not be disgraced, in the name of Jesus.

Chapter 27

YOUR DREAMS REVEAL SPIRITUAL ACTIVITY CONCERNING YOU

Dreams are a monitoring system of the spiritual realm. Dreams are a spiritual communication system between the physical and the spiritual realm. You want your dreams clear, since they are a spiritual way of communication with the physical realm. Sometimes, God talks to His people through dreams: *"And he said, Hear now my words: If there be a prophet among you, I the LORD will make myself known unto him in a vision, and will speak unto him in a dream." —Numbers 12:6. "And it shall come to pass afterward, that I will pour out my spirit upon all flesh; and your sons and your daughters shall prophesy, your old men shall dream dreams, your young men shall see visions." —Joel 2:28 NKJV.*

Before going to bed, cover your dreams in the blood of Jesus. Ask God to speak and give you prophetic dreams.

As God communicates with us in dreams, the demonic also uses dreams to access our lives, and release their evil. Satan is counterfeit of the good that God is. *"But while men slept, his enemy came and sowed tares among the wheat, and went his way." —Matthew 13:25.*

Here are some of the things that can open the door for demonic dreams.

Enemy conflict comes against us for two reasons; both are because the LORD allows it. The first reason is that we are called to be overcomers and put darkness under our feet—we are warriors. The second, the negative one, is that our lifestyles honor ungodliness and therefore open demonic doors. If we heed the chastening of demonic dreams, we can repent and change and thus overcome evil with good.

"He who overcomes shall inherit all things, and I will be his God and he shall be my son."—Revelation 21:7. "When you lie down, you will not be afraid; yes, you will lie down and your sleep will be sweet."—Proverbs 3:24 NKJV. "After this I awoke and looked around, and my sleep was sweet to me."—Jeremiah 31:26 NKJV.

The enemy will come while men sleep at night, to steal, to kill, and to destroy. When you dream any evil dream, you must get up and pray, and cancel every assignment of the enemy against you—that it shall not prosper. Pray, *"Thus saith the LORD GOD, It shall not stand, neither shall it come to pass."—Isaiah 7:7.* Immediately make that declaration that it shall not stand and it shall not happen in your life, in the name of Jesus.

Fasting is a great way to reverse evil dreams. You can fast for a day, or three days. While fasting, focus on praying that God will not allow that evil dream to happen in your life. While fasting, whenever you feel hunger, open your mouth and reject that evil dream, cancel it by the blood of Jesus, and release the blessings and protection of God over you and your family, in Jesus' name. You can also read some spiritual warfare chapters such as *Psalms 35, 25, 27, 140, and 91,* which are powerful and will cancel any attack of the enemy against you.

Because we are spirit and soul that live in a body, dreams are the channel of communication with the spiritual realm. We must live in a way that keeps our spirit man strong, so we are not the victims of the demonic attacks in dreams. When we are not paying attention to the things of God, we can miss His instruction or warning. We invite trouble in the spirit when we choose entertainment that is impure, violent and carnal. *"Those who walk righteously and speak uprightly, who despise the gain of oppression, who wave away a bribe instead of accepting it, who stop their ears from hearing of bloodshed and shut their eyes from looking on evil, they will live on the heights; their refuge will be the fortresses of rocks; their food will be supplied, their water assured."—Isaiah 33:15-16 NRS.*

We invite trouble in the spirit when we do not guard what our eyes see. *"The lamp of the body is the eye. If therefore your eye is good, your whole body will be full of light. But if your eye is bad, your whole body will be full of darkness. If therefore the light that is in you is darkness, how great is that darkness!" —Matthew 6:22-23.*

Pay attention to any regular dream. A reoccurring dream may be warning you of problems to come, giving you a solution or promise of blessings. The devil is the one behind evil dreams. Dreams from God are usually colorful, peaceful, promising, and clear. Dreams from the devil are usually scary causing you to awaken with unrest and fear. Some of the ways the enemy works in dreams against us are: eating with the dead, trouble while swimming in water, serving people you do not know, animal attacks, and marriage in the spirit world with unknown men or women. Additionally, the enemy is the source of dreams about having children in the spirit world, having sexual intercourse with known or unknown partners, getting out of the body for meetings, forceful sex or feeding, and regular drinking of red liquid.

When you have these kinds of dreams, you must pray when you wake up. If you do not remember your dreams, it is best to cancel any evil dream and receive the good dreams. Job was attacked in his dreams: *"When I think my bed will comfort me and my couch will ease my complaint, even then you frighten me with dreams and terrify me with visions." —Job 7:13-14 NIV. "For God speaketh once, yea twice, yet man perceiveth it not." —Job 33:14.*

God spoke to Abraham in the dream in *Genesis 15:12*, and in *Genesis 37*, God shows Joseph his destiny in a dream.

Keep your life holy and close to God. Do not go to bed angry and open the door for the demonic.

> *"Quench not the Spirit. Despise not prophesyings. Prove all things; hold fast that which is good. Abstain from all appearance of evil. And the very God of peace sanctify you wholly; and I pray God your whole spirit and soul and body be preserved blameless unto the coming of our Lord Jesus Christ. Faithful is he that calleth you, who also will do it." —1 Thessalonians 5:19-24.*

A reoccurring dream may be warning you of problems to come, giving you a solution or promise of blessings.

When dreams are from God there is no fear, there is assurance to bless you.

A dream can be used to alert you, and dreams from God could be to comfort you. In a dream, an angel appeared to Mary's husband Joseph, to tell him that Jesus was the son of God. *"But while he thought on these things, behold, the angel of the LORD appeared unto him in a dream, saying, Joseph, thou son of David, fear not to take unto thee Mary thy wife: for that which is conceived in her is of the Holy Ghost."—Matthew 1:20.* God gave the wise men a warning: *"And being warned of God in a dream that they should not return to Herod, they departed into their own country another way."—Matthew 2:12.* Pilate's wife had a dream about Jesus, and warned her husband: *"When he was set down on the judgment seat, his wife sent unto him, saying, Have thou nothing to do with that just man: for I have suffered many things this day in a dream because of him."—Matthew 27:19.*

Prayer Points—Open your mouth and pray

✛ Pray and ask the LORD to make you strong spiritually. LORD, by Your great power, may You always give me warning of what to be aware of, in the name of Jesus.

✛ LORD, bless me with good communication lines with You in my dreams; show me things to come in my dreams, in the name of Jesus.

God talked to Solomon in his dreams giving great promises: *"In Gibeon the LORD appeared to Solomon in a dream by night: and God said, Ask what I shall give thee."—1 Kings 3:5.*

✛ Father, bless me with dreams with good promises, as You did Solomon. Let my dreams bring the blessings of God into my life, in the name of Jesus.

✛ Holy Ghost, fill me that I might bring forth glory to God, in the name of Jesus.

✛ Let the anointing for victory and overcoming fall upon me through my dreams, in the name of Jesus.

✞ Let all evil dreams be nullified, reversed, and conquered, in the name of Jesus. I cancel them. I forbid them from manifesting, in the name of Jesus.

✞ Holy Ghost, purge my system and my blood from satanic foods and injections.

✞ I break every evil covenant and initiation through dreams. I renounce and denounce all evil associations in my dreams, in the name of Jesus.

✞ LORD Jesus, replace all satanic dreams with heavenly visions and divinely inspired dreams.

✞ Blood of Jesus wash all the organs in my body that may have been attacked in my dream, in the name of Jesus.

✞ Confess these scriptures aloud: *Psalms 27:1-2*, *1 Corinthians 10:21*, and *Psalms 91*.

✞ Let all evil dreams be replaced with blessings, in the name of Jesus.

✞ I command all my good dreams to become a reality in my life, in the name of Jesus.

✞ I claim back all the good things I have lost because of defeat and attacks in my dreams, in Jesus' name.

✞ I recover my stolen virtues, goodness, and blessings, in Jesus' name.

✞ I receive healing for every area of my body that has been inflicted in the dream, in the mighty name of Jesus.

✞ I destroy all satanic manipulations through dreams, in Jesus' name.

✞ I reject every evil spiritual load placed on me through dreams, in Jesus' name.

Chapter 28

BREAKING CURSES

A curse is an utterance that will invoke a supernatural power to inflict harm or release punishment on someone or something. Curses can be invoke by solemn utterances, or can be self-inflicted by casual statements like, "Oh, I am so stupid!" Both of these are effective against your life. Words are powerful.

An evil priest, witch, or any power of darkness can curse a person with evil words. Curses can manifest in many ways, including sickness, poverty, oppression, and being unable to hold on to good things in life—provoking constant failure in areas where a person should be getting blessings and success. A cursed person will tend to experience constant tragedies and loses. They experience constant failure at edge of breakthrough and regular disappointment.

This does not mean every difficult situation we go through is due to curses. God sometimes leads us through challenges to bring us through and bring us out to a better place. The LORD allows His children to experience things that are hard, and may be painful, but we come out stronger in faith, better in character, more humble, more patience, and more dependent on God. In those hard times, we tend to feel and appreciate the goodness of God more. God is close to the broken hearted. Everything a believer goes through will eventually work out for the good of that person as decreed, *"And we know that all things work together for good to them that love God, to them who are the called according to his purpose."* —Romans 8:28.

If you are affected by a curse such as listed above, God has good news for you. Accept Jesus as your Savior. You can be free from demonic oppression and have authority over the devil and his curses instead of his spirits having power over you or your family. The scripture says, *"...and [Jesus] gave them power and authority over all devils, and to cure diseases."* —*Luke 9:1 NKJV.*

Can a curse affect a Christian?

We are redeemed from the curse, but if we open the door for the enemy by living a life of constant disobedience to God, that disobedience opens the door for devil to come in. If you give Satan a foothold, he will take a stronghold. Satan is always looking for ways to come into our lives and carry out his evil plans, which include curses. Paul was writing to Christians when he said, *"...not give the devil any foothold, or a place"* —*Ephesians 4:27 NIV.*

Curses can work against a believer who is living a double life not fully sold out to God. We give our power and authority away when we live in the flesh all the time. If we are not walking in love, it makes it easy for the devil to work on us. If we walk in love, "Love conquers all." If we are not operating in faith, we expose ourselves to the enemies' devices, *"...for whatsoever [is] not of faith is sin."* — *Romans 14:23.*

If we do our best to live for God every day, even when we fall short, and repent, it makes it very hard for the enemy to prevail in cursing us. *"...An undeserved curse will not land on its intended victim."* —*Proverbs 26:2 NLT.*

The story of Balaam and Israel gives us a good example of this principle in *Numbers 22.* Balak sent for Balaam, to come and curse the children of Israel, so he could overcome them. Balaam could not do it, but instead he kept blessing them. No force can bring curses on us when we honor God with our lives. God will turn those curses into blessings.

The first step towards breaking curses is to repent of sins that may have opened the door to them. It may not have been your own sin directly, it could be a parent or ancestor. You must repent for their sins also, because they are your bloodline. *"The LORD is slow to anger, abounding in love and forgiving sin and rebellion. Yet he does not leave the guilty unpunished; he punishes the children for the sin of the parents to the third and fourth generation."* —*Numbers 14:18 NIV.* Thank God there is forgiveness after repentance! After forgiveness, you can pray, cancel all curses, and start enjoying the blessings of the LORD.

> *You can be free from demonic oppression and have authority over the devil and his curses*

Prayer Points—Open your mouth and pray

✟ I command every curse that has entered my life through the laying on of hands, words, sex, evil dedication, and inherited infirmities, to be forever broken and destroyed. I am released from every bondage—no more oppression, in Jesus' name.

✟ From today, every abnormality in our lives shall receive divine order, by the power of God.

✟ Any curse operating upon any organ of my body is now rendered null and void, in the name of Jesus.

✟ By Your great power, LORD, I cancel all forms of deformity and infirmity, in the name of Jesus.

✟ The LORD is Spirit. Where the Spirit of the LORD is, there is liberty; I release myself from every evil spirit programming me for failure, in Jesus' name.

✟ Every curse of disappointment and failure is cancelled by the blood of Jesus.

✟ Every curse of poverty, fired into my life through evil wickedness, is turned into a blessing, in Jesus' name.

✟ May the divine, creative power of God reproduce and replace any and every thing taken or damaged in your life by any form of curse, in the name of Jesus.

"He shall come unto us as the rain, as the latter and former rain unto the earth."—Hosea 6:3.

✟ The rain of God is the blessing of God, so I command every evil umbrella to burn because it is preventing my rain. I shall receive rain of peace, mercy, joy, grace and goodness, in the name of Jesus.

✟ Let every spirit controlling deeply rooted problems in my life through soul tie covenants break now, by the blood of Jesus.

✞ I am no longer a victim—I am a victor. God is much more than everything that has held me bound. He is bigger than the biggest, higher than the highest, mightier than the mightiest. God is more than everything in Heaven and on Earth— He is so much more. You are free from evil. Hallelujah!

"I am the LORD thy God which teach thee to profit, which lead thee by the way that you should go."—Isaiah 48:17. Your life is now led by the LORD. Praise God.

✞ From Dr. Pat: Let every problem that has held you bound be broken right now. Be released and set free in Jesus' name. You are free. *"If the Son therefore shall make you free, ye shall be free indeed."—John 8:36 NKJV.*

Chapter 29

DELIVERANCE FROM WITCHCRAFT SPIRITS

Witchcraft should not been given any chance to bring evil into our lives, homes, schools, churches, and communities. God is not pleased with witches.

> *"Now the works of the flesh are manifest, which are these; Adultery, fornication, uncleanness, lasciviousness, Idolatry, witchcraft, hatred, variance, emulations, wrath, strife, seditions, heresies, Envyings, murders, drunkenness, reveling, and such like: of the which I tell you before, as I have also told you in time past, that they which do such things shall not inherit the kingdom of God." — Galatians 5:19-21 NKJV.*

The Bible says, *"Thou shalt not suffer a witch to live."* — *Exodus 22:18.*

Witches are those practicing evil magic, cultic power; they engage in black magic to harm or murder others, through spells, incantations and so forth. People get into witchcraft for power and are sometimes deceived about what it really is. They may be promised power, prosperity, and all kinds of good things if they get into witchcraft. The witchcraft promise to people does not deliver. Instead, the door opens for all kinds of evil in their lives and the lives of people around them. The Bible warns us about it, *"Let no one be found among you who engages in witchcraft." — Deuteronomy 18:10-11 NKJV.*

God hates witchcraft with perfect hatred. Because witches are wicked, they release evil decrees and curses on innocent people. Witches release curses upon people deemed to be in their way, people they are jealous of, or others for no reason at all. Witchcraft causes many problems. Witches are agents of the devil. A witch is a practitioner of witchcraft. Witchcraft is counterfeit spiritual authority. It is using evil spirits to dominate, manipulate, or control others. One of the expressed goals of this movement is to destroy God's creation. Many Christians are presently suffering some form of attack from those who practice witchcraft. Discern the nature of these attacks, and know how to overcome them.

Understanding Satan's devices significantly increases our advantage in the battle. I was scheduled to preach with another pastor a few years ago. She told us how her sister's daughter, who was about five years old, had died suddenly. She and the family went to the hospital and were praying for this little girl. While they were praying, she heard the LORD say, "call her fire," she said, she called her fire. The moment she called her fire, the little girl sneezed, and she was fine. A couple of weeks later, the

> Witchcraft is counterfeit spiritual authority.

young lady who was the pastor's maid confessed that she was into witchcraft and had presented the little girl into the witchcraft realm to be killed for a sacrifice. She went on to say, "The moment you started praying and called her fire, we had to put back all the body parts that was already prepared and divided to be eaten. We could not eat fire." So I encourage you, when you feel demonic attacks against your body, pray calling on the Holy Ghost fire to take over your body and cover your body with the blood of Jesus.

Witchcraft has caused a lot of problems and tragedies in the lives of many innocent souls. Lives have been cut short and sent to the grave earlier than God's original plan for them. Witchcraft has caused marriages to be destroyed, financial problems, sickness, failures of all kinds, and trouble in all areas. Witchcraft attacks make life difficult for innocent people. They cause people to be unable to hold on to good things in their lives: jobs, relationships, marriages, finances and so forth. They cause problems such as addictions, limitations, delays, and hindrances. The way to overcome evil powers is praying the Word of God, using the name of Jesus and the blood of Jesus. *"They overcome him by the blood of the Lamb and the word of their testimony."—Revelation 12:11 NKJV.*

Prayer Points—Open your mouth and pray

✛ Every arrow of witchcraft fired into my life, backfire, in the name of Jesus.

✛ Every decree of impossibility by witchcraft against my life, be revoked and die, in the name of Jesus.

"We are not to be ignorant of the enemy's devices."—2 Corinthians 2:11 NKJV.

✛ Father, by Your great power, I shall not be ignorant of the enemy's devices. LORD, expose every evil plan against me, and cause them all to fail, in the name of Jesus.

"Be sober, be vigilant; because your adversary the devil, as a roaring lion, walks about, seeking whom he may devour. But resist him, steadfast in faith..."—1 Peter 5:8-9 NKJV.

✛ Father, in the name of Jesus, make me aware of every enemy around me, every demonic device against me, and every assignment against me. I break any power exerted against me in the name of Jesus. I come against that counterfeit authority with the true authority of the name of Jesus.

"In thee, O LORD, do I put my trust; let me never be ashamed: deliver me in thy righteousness. Bow down thine ear to me; deliver me speedily: be thou my strong rock, for an house of defense to save me. For thou art my rock and my fortress therefore for thy name's sake lead me, and guide me."—Psalms 31:1-3.

✚ Let my trust in God deliver me from shame. I receive the grace not to be disgraced. LORD, hear me and deliver me speedily. Father, do not delay to answer my prayer. Father, You are my strong rock, my defense. Thank You, LORD, that You fight all my battles, in the name of Jesus.

✚ Father, disconnect me from every evil point of contact. May the LORD expose and remove all evil plans from my life and the lives of my loved ones, in the name of Jesus.

✚ Many times, there are powers behind some of the problems we are facing.

✚ Almighty God, let every power behind my problems fail, let them all be frustrated and disappointed, in the name of Jesus.

✚ I cover myself with the blood of Jesus and bind every cultic power. I cover everyzthing that belongs to me with the blood of Jesus Christ.

✚ The blood of Jesus is in my spirit, soul and my body, therefore I destroy every evil in my life, in Jesus' name.

"As for the head of those who surround me, Let the evil of their lips cover them; Let burning coals fall upon them; Let them be cast into the fire, Into deep pits, that they rise not up again. Let not a slanderer be established in the earth; Let evil hunt the violent man to overthrow him..."—Psalms 140:9-11 NKJV.

✚ I come against the head of the powers coming against me, I reverse all their assignments against my life, they shall not prosper. I overcome every work of the devil, in Jesus' name.

✚ Holy Ghost fire, take over my life as I pray this prayer today, burn everything that is not of You in my life. Set me free from every witchcraft activity.

✚ Almighty God, turn my prayer today to fire, and turn every witchcraft power to wood. Let them be consumed, in the name of Jesus. LORD, turn every witchcraft activity in my life to nothing.

"But cowards, unbelievers, the corrupt, murderers, the immoral, those who practice witchcraft, idol worshipers, and all liars—their fate is in the fiery lake of burning sulfur. This is the second death."—Revelation 21:8.

✞ Witchcraft power operates in some families. They can be responsible for most destruction in that family.

✞ Every witchcraft stronghold in my family be destroyed by fire, in the name of Jesus.

✞ Almighty God, visit my family with Your power and deliver us from every witchcraft attack, bondage, sickness, and poverty.

✞ All blessings diverted by witches, I command you to return. The blood of Jesus delivers all who are tormented by witchcraft, in the mighty name of Jesus.

✞ I command my destiny and the destiny of my loved ones to be released from every witchcraft attack, in the name of our Lord Jesus Christ.

✞ Every kind of damage done by witchcraft be repaired by the blood of Jesus, this year, from person to person, in Jesus' name.

"He sent his word, and healed them, and delivered them from their destructions."—Psalms 107:20.

✞ May the Word of God heal me of all witchcraft attacks, and deliver me from all destruction from their assignment, in the name of Jesus. My life shall move forward and succeed contrary to witchcraft decrees, in the name of Jesus.

✞ My ministry and calling shall move forward and succeed contrary to witchcraft decrees.

✞ Contrary to witchcraft plans, I shall not weep over my family, and my family shall not weep over me, in the name of Jesus.

✞ Every good thing the witchcraft spirit has delayed in my life, come forth quickly, there shall be no more delay to my fulfillment, in Jesus' name.

"The Anointing Destroys the Yoke."
—*Isaiah 10:27 NKJV.*

✞ Let all evil yokes in my life be destroyed. Yoke of sickness evaporate and yoke of failure be cancelled. I forever reject and forbid all enemies yokes, in the name of Jesus.

✞ Evil spells against my life, be revoked by the blood of Jesus.

✞ Every witchcraft spirit expecting me to fail, Father, disapprove and disappoint them, in the name of Jesus.

✞ By the fire of God, I command every witchcraft power to release my blessings, in the name of Jesus. Release the blessings of my loved ones now, by the great power of God.

✞ Witchcraft battles and attacks at the edge of my breakthrough, at the edge of my success, perish today. I shall no longer be disappointed at the edge of breakthrough; I shall no longer fail at the edge of my miracle, in the name of Jesus.

✞ Every witchcraft padlock fashioned against my progress, break by fire, in the name of Jesus.

✞ Any power taking my blessing, let God arise and stop them forever, and restore, with interest, everything good they have deprived me of, in the name of Jesus.

✞ Every evil power of witchcraft standing at the door of my blessing, your time has expired. I command you to move and let me through to my place of success. You shall no longer hold me back from going through those doors, in Jesus' name.

✞ Father God, deliver me from all ignorance, deliver me from lack of knowledge, and help me confront whatever needs to be corrected in my life, in the name of Jesus. Disappointment, I command you vanish from my life in the name of Jesus.

✞ Father God, let the best things in life be given to me: elevation, peace, favor, joy, health prosperity and good relationships, in the mighty name of Jesus.

Chapter 30

SILENCING THE VOICES
OF EVIL ALTARS

An altar is a platform, a table, or elevated place on which a priest places an offering and makes a petition or even a demand. This can be an altar of God or of the devil. All altars are erected for a purpose, to carry out wills. Altars can bring victories or defeats.

Both good and evil powers behind altars respond to sacrifices offered to them. Our Heavenly Father is the good power, and Satan is the evil power. In *1 Samuel 7:7-11*, Samuel made a sacrifice for the children of Israel to win the battle against the Philistines. The cross of Jesus is the only acceptable altar. The power in the cross cancels all evil altars, but we must tap into the power of the cross and cancel altars erected against us for evil.

> *"And he cried against the altar in the word of the LORD, and said, O altar, altar, thus saith the LORD; Behold, a child shall be born unto the house of David, Josiah by name; and upon thee shall he offer the priests of the high places that burn incense upon thee, and men's bones shall be burnt upon thee."—1 Kings 13:2.*

An altar is a place of deliberations, decisions, and even dedications—whether for blessings or curses. An altar is a place of covenant and sacrifice—a place of spiritual traffic. When Jacob saw angels ascending and descending in his dream, it was there that God made a covenant with him and he built an altar for the LORD.

Any time evil is determined against someone; an evil priest will go to their altar and make a sacrifice and a petition or demand. They will sometimes use blood by making animal or even human sacrifices. The priest establishes a point of contact with the person they are trying to curse or attack spiritually by calling out their full name, making an image of that person with something like a doll, using a mirror to access the person, or use the person's clothing, hair, blood, or other personal possession.

Prayer Points—Open your mouth and pray

✠ If you are the victim of an evil altar, here is the way out.

✠ Repent of anything you have done to make any evil altar prosper in your life, and also seek forgiveness for the sins of your ancestors that may be affecting your life today.

✠ Father, forgive every sin that has opened the door for an evil altar to prosper in my life. *LORD*, by Your mercy, I pray that You forgive my sins, the sins of my parents, and the sins of my ancestors. I pray for forgiveness for every sin in my blood line, in the name of Jesus.

✠ I renounce and denounce the hold of all evil altars over my life, by the blood of Jesus Christ.

✠ I withdraw whatever they are using to represent me in the evil altar. I resist their will over me, by the Word of God. I override all evil pronunciation against me with the Word of God and the blood of Jesus.

✠ I command all the voices from evil altars to no longer speak into my life, and decree that my life will no longer respond to those evil altars, in the name of Jesus.

✠ With the blood of Jesus Christ, I destroy that evil altar working against my family and me, in Jesus' name.

✠ Make your confession against evil altars, declaring that Jesus is the Lord of your life; therefore, no evil altar has the power to speak into your life anymore. Nullify every legal ground the enemy has used to access your life, by the blood of Jesus and in Jesus' name.

✞ By the power in the blood of Jesus, I release myself from the bondage of evil altars, in the name of Jesus.

✞ Every evil altar erected against my life, I forever silence you, by the name and blood of Jesus.

✞ I command evil priests and their altars working against my life to be consumed by the fire of God.

✞ My life will now receive repair from all damage done by an evil altar, in the name of Jesus. Repair physically, mentally, spiritually, emotionally, relationally and financially, in the name of Jesus.

"Is not my word like fire," declares the LORD, "and like a hammer that breaks a rock in pieces?"
—Jeremiah 23:29 NKJV.

✞ Let the Word of God set every evil altar ablaze, in the name of Jesus. Let the Word be a hammer and break to pieces all evil altars working and speaking against my life, in the name of Jesus.

✞ Let the thunder of God smite every evil priest and the altar from which they are working against me, in the name of Jesus.

✞ By the blood of Jesus, I withdraw my blessings from every evil altar. I command restoration in all areas of my life, in the name of Jesus.

✞ Almighty God, send Your angels to withdraw our glory and virtue from the demonic altars and give them back to us, in the name of Jesus.

✞ I command any breakthroughs held up on the satanic altar to be released to us now—no more delay, in Jesus' name.

✞ I command all my blessings diverted away from me by evil altars to be returned to me now, in the mighty name of Jesus.

✞ Every weapon formed against me from the

> *I destroy that evil altar working against my family and me, in Jesus' name.*

demonic altar shall not prosper and must be condemned by the blood of Jesus.

✟ I withdraw everything that is rightfully mine from the evil altar, in the name of Jesus.

✟ From now on, no evil imagined against me shall prosper, in the name of Jesus. It is written, *"...affliction shall not rise up the second time"—Nahum 1:9*, therefore I forbid any evil from coming back into my life in any area, after these prayers, in the name of Jesus.

✟ I am permanently set free from all attacks from evil altars, in Jesus' mighty name. Amen!

OPEN

YOUR

MOUTH

AND

PRAY!

CPSIA information can be obtained
at www.ICGtesting.com
Printed in the USA
BVHW070740240821
615015BV00006B/921